D1594236

The Kwangju Uprising

The Kwangju Uprising

Shadows over the Regime in South Korea

edited by
Donald N. Clark

Westview Press / Boulder and London

Westview Special Studies on East Asia

This Westview softcover edition is printed on acid-free paper and bound in softcovers that carry the highest rating of the National Association of State Textbook Administrators, in consultation with the Association of American Publishers and the Book Manufacturers' Institute.

Copyright © 1988 by Westview Press, Inc.

Published in 1988 in the United States of America by Westview Press, Inc.; Frederick A. Praeger, Publisher; 5500 Central Avenue, Boulder, Colorado 80301

Library of Congress Cataloging-in-Publication Data
Clark, Donald N.
  The Kwangju uprising.
  (Westview special studies on East Asia)
  Bibliography: p.
  Includes index.
  1. Kwangju Uprising, Korea (South), 1980. I. Title.
II. Series.
DS925.K86C53 1988   951.9′5043   87-27419
ISBN 0-8133-7523-1

Printed and bound in the United States of America

⬤ The paper used in this publication meets the requirements of the American National Standard for
    Permanence of Paper for Printed Library Materials Z39.48-1984.

6   5   4   3   2   1

Contents

vi

The Kwangju Uprising:
An Introduction

Donald N. Clark

When Kim Chae-gyu, Director of the KCIA, the Korean Central Intelligence Agency, assassinated President Park Chung Hee on the night of October 26, 1979, South Korea was plunged into a period of volatile political change. Despite the declaration of martial law that followed the assassination, many Koreans thought the moment might also be a time to dismantle the late president's system of ruling by decree and to revive Korea's democratic institutions. The continuing North Korean threat made it necessary to maintain a huge military establishment in the South, and some degree of military influence in politics was inevitable; yet many Koreans hoped that with time and prosperity their country had matured beyond the point where a military coup was likely. Given the uncertainties, however, most people held back, watching as the powerholders in government, business, and the military jockeyed for influence.

Eighteen years of the Park regime had wrought fundamental changes in the power structure of South Korea. By 1979 the military was stronger than ever, officered by veterans of the Vietnam War, and although Park had succeeded in keeping the armed forces under control during his years in power, there was no one else who could command loyalty throughout the service hierarchies.

Other power centers had developed as well. The economy had grown enormously giving rise to the chaebol, major business enterprises such as Hyundai, Daewoo, and the Lucky-Goldstar Group, which were powering Korea's emergence as a major trading nation. Park's government had gathered political power in Ch'ongwa-dae, the "Blue House," and from there an administrative staff ran the executive branch, the secret police (the KCIA), the ruling Democratic Republican Party (DRP), and through it the National Assembly. A drastic

1

change in the constitution, adopted in 1972 with virtually no public debate or discussion, had given Park the authority to maintain himself in office indefinitely by creating an electoral college that was dominated by his own appointees and party members. This and other elements of the 1972 constitutional revision known collectively as the "Revitalizing Reforms," or Yushin system, followed Park's near-loss of the presidential election of 1971. In that election, Park's opponent, Kim Dae Jung of South Cholla Province, won 45.3 percent of the popular vote. To remove the possibility of having to stand for popular election again, in 1972 Park asserted that the security situation in Northeast Asia was too fluid to permit disunity in the Republic. Arguing that tighter controls were necessary to cope with the shift in American policy that came with Richard Nixon's opening to China, as well as the dramatic new dialogue between Seoul and P'yongyang which began in July 1972, Park began ruling by emergency decree. Using the successive economic and security crises that followed throughout the 1970s as justification, he simply continued ruling by decree until his death.

During the Yushin years of the seventies, an articulate opposition developed in the universities and churches. Students, who traditionally have been the most visible and vocal sector of the opposition, continued their demonstrations against each new restriction under the Yushin policy. Opposition leader Kim Dae Jung went abroad, mustering support for the anti-Yushin movement among overseas Koreans until the KCIA kidnapped him from a Tokyo hotel, came close to murdering him, and finally brought him back to Korea under permanent house arrest. The leading independent issues magazine, Sasanggye (The World of Thought), was ordered closed after it published works by the dissident poet Kim Chi-ha. In 1974, when the KCIA blocked advertising in the independent newspaper Tong-a Ilbo, thousands of people took out private ads to help keep the paper going until, finally, new press decrees put KCIA agents in the editorial rooms of all newspapers to exercise prior censorship. In 1976 the opposition raised the stakes by issuing a public manifesto demanding an end to the Yushin system—and saw its leaders harassed and imprisoned.

After the unruly American withdrawal from Vietnam in 1975, the Korean government argued ever more strongly that national security required Yushin-type limits on dissent. With more than a touch of Confucian disdain for disunity and discord, the Park government habitually equated democratic opposition with "anti-state" attitudes. Under the existing national security laws, it was easy for the state to label anyone active in the opposition a security risk and traitor.

Park Chung Hee's government used economic growth to purchase public toleration for the Yushin system of government. From the early 1970's Korea's GNP grew at rates exceeding ten percent. There was a clear rise in the standard of living. Though most Korean workers were not able to enjoy the full benefits of Korean modernization, especially in the early years, by the mid-1970's there were real gains being made. The early Park-era exhortation to "Produce! Export! Build!" was bringing results. In the rural areas of Korea, the Saemaul ("New Community") Movement, was bringing improvements in the lives of farmers.

Korea's growth, however, was vulnerable to changes in the climate of international financing, since so much of it was financed by debt, and energy supplies, since Korea imported virtually all of its petroleum. The military was a constant drain on the budget, the more so because of the shifting pattern of U.S. aid from grants to loans and sales.

The energy crises and inflation of the seventies helped cause dislocations in the Korean economy and work force. Workers' wages were kept at a controlled low level to keep Korean manufactured goods competitive in the international marketplace. By the late 1970's, when it was obvious that members of the business elite were enjoying great profits while ordinary workers could barely feed their families and were forbidden to organize unions or engage in effective collective bargaining, labor disturbances, which once had been sporadic, became frequent. Fanned by serious inflation, by mid-1979 the labor unrest had developed into more and more frequent sit-downs, walkouts, demonstrations, and strikes. By October the government was no longer able to control the outbreaks with its normal tactics of intimidation and tear gas. Some in the government argued for more severe repression--bullets and martial law if necessary. Others urged conciliation. Park Chung Hee died, literally, in the crossfire between these two points of view, as KCIA Director Kim Chae-gyu, convinced that the President was planning to use the more brutal tactics advocated by his advisor and bodyguard Cha Chi-ch'ol, pulled out his pistol and shot them both to death.

It was characteristic of Park that he had made little provision for a successor. It was a favorite spectator sport in Seoul during most of his tenure to witness the rise and fall of various heirs-apparent as Park played them off against each other. As a result there was considerable ill-will among the factions representing the Blue House, the

KCIA, and the military. When Park died on October 26, the situation was thus thrown into confusion. The State Council immediately ordered the declaration of martial law. Ch'oe Kyu-ha, a senior official and former Prime Minister, was elevated to Acting President. KCIA Director Kim Chae-gyu, was immediately arrested. The Martial Law Command ordered an investigation to determine whether there had been a conspiracy, and to find out who else was involved. To head the investigation the Martial Law Commander, General Chong Sung-hwa, named Major General Chun Doo Hwan, chief of the Army Security Command, the military version (and sometime rival) of the civilian KCIA. The story of Korean politics in late 1979 and early 1980 is the chronicle of General Chun's rise to power against all odds and obstacles, to emerge as President of the Fifth Republic, anointed during his state visit to the United States in early 1981 by President Ronald Reagan as a key defender of freedom's frontier.

For several weeks after Park's assassination, despite martial law, there was great hope within Korea that the Yushin decrees would be replaced with a more responsive democratic system. Many felt that Korea had grown and matured politically to the point where mere force was not enough to legitimize the exercise of power. The people would not permit a regression to rule by a military junta. The military itself was part of this mature emerging nation, and shared the people's yearning for freedom from the terror and tension of the Yushin years.

However, on December 12, 1979 General Chun seized control of the armed forces in a bloody night-time coup. Through the spring of 1980 he maneuvered his most trusted fellow-officers, many of them classmates in the eleventh class of the Korean Military Academy (1955), into key positions of power. He assumed the directorate of the KCIA in April. The continuing public outcry against dictatorship in the Blue House became a rising public outcry against Chun's steady erosion of hopes for democratic reform, taking the form of demonstrations and labor actions, and pointing toward an inevitable confrontation between the newly-emerging military government and the people. Finally in May, in the city of Kwangju in South Cholla Province, a most serious confrontation did occur. It involved growing demonstrations, a citizens' revolt against military special forces "Black Berets," an expulsion of government forces from the city, and the forcible recapture of the city by regular army troops. The United States may or may not have played a role in releasing the troops from the joint US-ROK Combined Forces Command for the reinvasion of Kwangju--the

U.S. claims it played no significant role, but large numbers of Koreans believe that the American decision-makers were at least indirectly involved. Many people were killed. The exact number is in dispute. The government says that 191 lives were lost. Other estimates range as high as 2,000.

In 1960, during the student-led April Revolution which toppled the regime of President Syngman Rhee, it was the civilian police who had turned their weapons on students and civilians. In April 1960 the Army won laurels from the people for its restraint in restoring order. As martial law was being declared on April 19, the crowds in Seoul had succeeded in driving the police from the streets. The fighting died down as martial law troops entered the city in the late afternoon and evening, and by the next day the army had peacefully taken control. In contrast with the police, the army refused to fire on demonstrators; and after April 20 the martial law commander refused to intrude on the political process. Instead the army allowed the combination of public outrage and American pressure to nudge President Rhee out of office, to be replaced by an interim president and eventually by a constitutionally elected government.

On April 20, 1960, as Seoul citizens were being allowed to climb aboard tanks parked at Kwanghwamun and pose for pictures, one had the sense that the ROK Army was an army of the people. Even after Park Chung Hee's cohort stepped in a year later to deal with the uncertainties created by the clumsy inefficiencies of democratic rule, many Koreans accepted the first coup as an inevitable, if not entirely desirable, measure. Park was able to persuade many Koreans that the army was doing its patriotic duty by restoring order.

This was not the case in 1980, by which time Chun Doo Hwan's cohorts in the army had demonstrated clearly their political ambitions. Kwangju proved that elements within the armed forces were willing to take the step of killing large numbers of Korean citizens in order to hold onto power.

After Kwangju the opposition to Chun was driven under ground, where much of it continues to smolder to this day. Chun and his colleagues went on to consolidate their power and to offer the general to the electoral college as the sole candidate for President in August. Claiming legitimacy from this process, Chun since then has presided over seven years of economic progress in Korea during which the promise of a better life has been realized by many more Korean people. At the same time, however, the acceptance of Chun as president has been sullen, at best. Kwangju has not been forgotten or forgiven. Neither has the United States been forgiven by many Koreans for the part it played, perhaps unwittingly, in paving the way for Chun to become the new South Korean strongman.

The main issue involving the United States is the allegation that General John A. Wickham, the Commander-in-Chief of the US-ROK Combined Forces Command, twice "allowed" Chun to use Korean components of the Combined Forces Command to promote his political ambitions—in December to seize the Defense Ministry and Army Headquarters, and in May to engage in the bloody recapture of Kwangju. The charge that American officials "allowed" or "encouraged" Chun to take power has given rise to something new—a palpable anti-Americanism in South Korea. Although a certain amount of anti-Americanism may be a natural byproduct of Korea's growing economic and political autonomy, the charge that Americans are partly responsible for reversing democratic trends in Korea is of concern and deserves to be examined.

If Kwangju refuted the claim to legitimacy of Chun Doo Hwan's regime, we need to know more about what really happened there. Koreans are not free to discuss the uprising and the government exhorts them to put it in the past. Yet campus demonstrations usually refer to it and have succeeded in keeping the memory of it alive. A key demand of the students who seized the United States Information Service building in Seoul in May 1985 was that there be a public hearing on Kwangju. Videotapes of foreign news broadcasts about Kwangju circulate fairly freely in Korea. Public curiosity was such in the summer of 1985 that the government was obliged to give a public accounting of the Kwangju incident to the National Assembly. The issue simply will not go away. If, as may yet be the case, Chun is succeeded in the presidency by former General Roh Tae Woo, who was a key participant in the events of 1979-1980, the wounds of Kwangju will not heal for many years to come.

American scholars of Korea, like other friends of the Korean people, were witnesses to the events of 1979-1980. As professionals in the field of Korean studies, we have an abiding interest in the lives of our Korean colleagues, and in the stance our government takes toward the Korean people.

This book is a collection of papers on Kwangju given in Boston at the April, 1987 meeting of the Association for Asian Studies. The authors, all Korea specialists, approached the uprising from varied academic perspectives. Anthropologist Linda Lewis was an eyewitness to the uprising, having been in Kwangju doing doctoral research when the incident occurred. David McCann of Cornell is a leading scholar and translator of Korean protest literature.

Historian Mark Peterson, Director of the Fulbright Program in Seoul at the time of the Kwangju uprising, presents analyses of recent interviews with the two American officials at the center of the controversy over the U.S. role, Ambassador William H. Gleysteen and General John A. Wickham. The panel had two discussants: Chong-Sik Lee of the University of Pennsylvania, a political scientist, and Donald Clark, of Trinity University, a historian. While preparing the book for production the authors agreed that a selection of supporting materials would be useful; hence the addition of a detailed chronology of the events surrounding the incident, drawn from a variety of sources, maps, and two documents: the South Korean Defense Ministry's official account of the Kwangju affair and the Combined Forces Command's own interpretation of the authority of the CFC Commander over Korean troops in peacetime.

The concept for the panel in Boston originated with Dr. Sung-il Choi of the Council for Korean Democracy, who worked for several years to get the scholarly community to confront the Kwangju issue and to discuss it openly. The authors are grateful for his inspiration and for the encouragement of colleagues Laurel Kendall, Donald Macdonald, David Steinberg, and Edward J. Baker III, among many others.

Participants in the project also wish to thank Westview Press and our editor, Susan McEachern, for her patient cooperation and assistance in getting the papers published. Thanks, too, to Eunice Nicholson at Trinity University for her cheerful and thoroughly professional performance of vital editorial tasks during production, and to Linda Clark for help with proofreading and indexing.

The opinions and conclusions in the various selections, of course, are those of the authors themselves.

KOREA

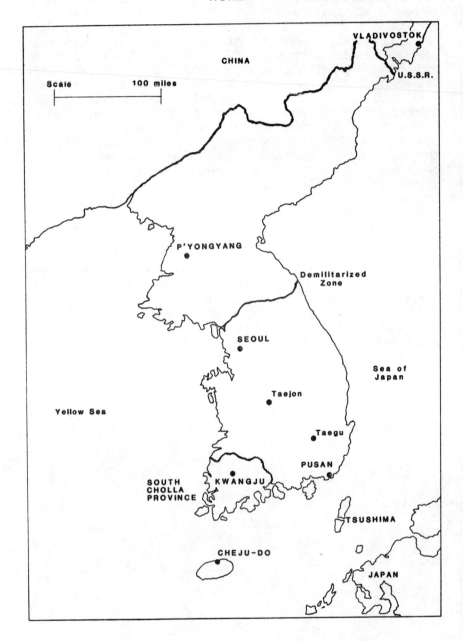

KWANGJU

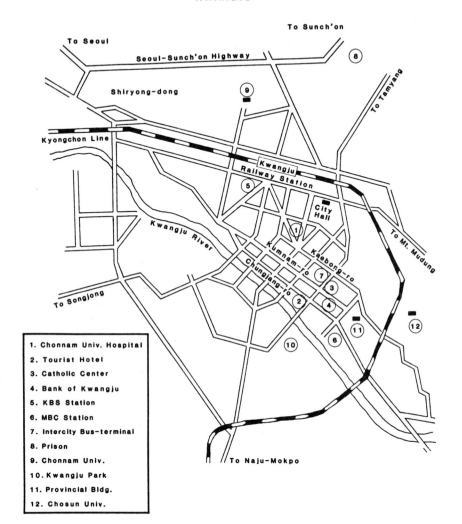

To Sunch'on

To Seoul

Seoul-Sunch'on Highway

Shiryong-dong

To Tamyang

8

9

Kyongchon Line

Kwangju Railway Station

5

City Hall

1

Kwangju River

Kumnam-ro

Kaebong-ro

Chungjang-ro

7

3

2

4

To Songjong

11

12

To Mt. Mudung

10

6

1. Chonnam Univ. Hospital
2. Tourist Hotel
3. Catholic Center
4. Bank of Kwangju
5. KBS Station
6. MBC Station
7. Intercity Bus-terminal
8. Prison
9. Chonnam Univ.
10. Kwangju Park
11. Provincial Bldg.
12. Chosun Univ.

To Naju-Mokpo

Chronology

1979

<u>Oct. 26</u>. President Park Chung Hee is assassinated by KCIA Director Kim Chae-gyu in the midst of growing demonstrations for democracy; martial law is imposed throughout South Korea except for Cheju Island; Prime Minister Ch'oe Kyu-ha becomes Acting President.

<u>Nov. 24</u>. 140 opposition movement leaders are arrested at a meeting at the Seoul YWCA calling for rapid democratization. Of these, a number are taken to the Army Security Command, headed by Major General Chun Doo Hwan, where they undergo torture.

<u>Dec. 7</u>. Acting President Ch'oe Kyu-ha is formally elected President by the electoral college.

<u>Dec. 8</u>. President Ch'oe lifts Park's Emergency Decree No. 9, which forbade criticism and dissent. Kim Dae Jung is freed from house arrest, where he had been since being released from a prison hospital in December 1978. Kim immediately calls for popular elections, says that "political and social chaos" might follow unless they are held soon. Amnesty for 68 other dissidents.

<u>Dec. 12</u>. Gen. Chun Doo Hwan leads a coup within the military; arrests General Chong Sung-hwa, the Army Chief of Staff, despite Pres. Ch'oe's refusal to sign the warrant; firefights develop between forces loyal to Chun and those loyal to Chong Sung-hwa and the government; Without checking with General John A. Wickham, US-ROK Combined Forces Commander, Chun sends for elements of the ROK Ninth Army Division under Gen. Roh Tae Woo. By 1:00 a.m. Defense

Minister No Che-hyon has signed the warrant for the arrest of General Chong Sung-hwa. Within a week Roh Tae Woo is appointed commander of the Seoul Garrison Command. Thirty or so older officers are replaced with military cohorts of Chun and Roh.

<u>Dec. 21</u>. Ch'oe Kyu-ha formally inaugurated President.

<u>Winter</u>. Many students expelled from school for dissident activities are reinstated. Political groups debate in the press and on television about a new constitutional system. The government agrees that President Ch'oe will be the government candidate in any future election. Kim Chae-gyu and four KCIA accomplices are tried and sentenced to death. Chong Sung-hwa is sentenced to ten years in prison for mishandling the assassination investigation. Kim Chae-gyu becomes the focus of some student rallies. There are many calls for his release.

1980
<u>Mar. 11</u>. General John A. Wickham, US-ROK Combined Forces Commander, is quoted in the <u>Asian Wall Street Journal</u> as saying that the South Korean military's proper role includes "being watch-dogs on political activity that could be destabilizing, and in a way making judgments about the eligibility and reliability of political candidates that may have some adverse influence on stability."

<u>Apr. 14</u>. General Chun Doo Hwan becomes acting director of the KCIA while continuing as head of the Army Security Command, although under South Korean law it is illegal for persons in the military to hold civilian positions.

<u>Mid-April</u>. Widespread campus demonstrations and labor strikes begin. Students call for campus reforms and reinstitution of student councils, which were banned during Park's presidency. Workers demand unpaid back wages and wage increases to help compensate for inflation, running at an annual rate of 89.2 percent for the first three months of 1980. After a violent strike in the southern coal-mining town of Sabuk, the government agrees to a 20 percent hike in wages. To hardliners in the military, this seems like a dangerous precedent.

<u>Early May</u>. Demonstrations continue to grow. Students begin peaceful, disciplined demonstrations off-campus calling for the end of martial law, resignation of Gen. Chun Doo Hwan,

and the abolition of compulsory off-campus military training. Education Minister Kim Ok-kil asks students if they want to repeat the experience of 1950, when untrained troops were slaughtered by the North Koreans. The students agree to continue reserve training.

May 15. Over 50,000 students demonstrate in downtown Seoul. Prime Minister Shin Hyon-hwak announces that the government will make concessions and try to speed democratization.

May 16. Students in Seoul call off demonstrations to await government's response. Kim Dae Jung and Kim Young-sam, opposition political leaders, meet and urge students to exercise "maximum self-restraint." In Kwangju, 35,000 students and citizens hold a peaceful torchlight procession and then call off further demonstrations.

May 17. Gen. Chun Doo Hwan reasserts military control. Nationwide martial law is declared. All political activity is banned. Universities are closed. National Assembly is barred from meeting (it was to have met on May 20, when a vote was expected to end the already-existing limited martial law). Criticism of present and past national leaders is forbidden. Hundreds of democratic leaders, politicians, students, and others are arrested, including opposition leader Kim Dae Jung. Also arrested is former Prime Minister Kim Chong-p'il, widely touted as a presidential contender.

May 18. In Kwangju, approximately 500 students demonstrate, demanding the end of martial law and the resignation of General Chun. Martial law troops reinforced by "Black Beret" paratroopers surround demonstrators and spectators and indiscriminately beat and bayonet them. Several dozen people are killed.

May 19. Military in Kwangju harass townspeople, singling out people at random, particularly those who appear to be students, for beatings and bayoneting. Shocked citizens join the student demonstrations, which occur in over 30 locations. The main streets are filled with tens of thousands of people. Many scores are killed, most of them unarmed civilians.

May 20. Word of paratrooper brutality spreads. Over 100,000 Kwangju citizens demonstrate; two radio stations are burned for broadcasting falsified news reports about the situation. Hospitals are completely filled. In Seoul, the military forces the Shin Hyon-Hwak cabinet to resign, in order to bear full responsibility for the Kwangju incident.

May 21. About 200,000 people demonstrate in Kwangju; city is sealed off by government troops. Army vehicles are commandeered by demonstrators; citizens obtain arms from police stations and army stockpiles; army retreats from city; telephone service is cut. At about midnight demonstrators take over the Provincial Administration Building. In Seoul, a new cabinet is appointed, all with close ties with the military. Members of the Korean Journalists Association stop work to protest arrests of members following their decision to defy censorship.

May 22. Citizens control Kwangju. Military accuses opposition leader Kim Dae Jung of sedition for allegedly instigating student demonstrators and rebellion in Kwangju--even though he was under arrest when it began. Ten thousand troops encircle Kwangju, while within the city people form a citizens council and begin negotiations with the military. Demonstrations spread to neighboring areas. The Pentagon announces that it has released four battalions of Korean troops under its control for use in suppressing the Kwangju demonstrations. According to one report, 500 people are reported dead in Kwangju, with 960 missing.

May 23. Hodding Carter, U.S. State Department spokesperson, announces to reporters that the Carter administration "has decided to support the restoration of security and order in South Korea while deferring pressure for political liberalization." Kwangju is orderly and quiet, and reportedly 85-95 percent of weapons have been turned in, at the request of the the the citizens committee. In Seoul, the military executes Kim Chae-gyu and four others convicted of conspiring to assassinate President Park.

May 24. 50,000 Kwangju residents demonstrate in the rain to protest martial law in spite of warnings from the martial law command. The army moves tanks into the edge of the city. Troops around the city stop anyone trying to enter or leave.

May 25. 30,000 people assemble in front of the Provincial Administration Building. Citizens council meets to formulate demands.

May 26. Citizens in Kwangju appeal to the U.S. government to help negotiate a truce.

May 27. The U.S. State Department declines to mediate, saying "We recognize that a situation of total disorder and disruption in a major city cannot be allowed to go on indefinitely." One hour later thousands of martial law troops invade Kwangju. Many persons are killed, the military regains control.

Aftermath. Martial law troops search house-to-house for participants in the demonstrations. Thousands of people are detained, interrogated, and released or arrested. Military suppresses accurate accounts of the situation. Numerous publications in the Cholla Provinces are banned. Kim Dae Jung and others are brought to trial on charges of sedition, with a possible death sentence.

End of May. The military forms a Special Committee for National Security Measures, with its largely-military Standing Committee chaired by Chun Doo Hwan, to coordinate policy among various government bodies. Chun confides to American journalist Robert Shaplen when questioned about his intentions, that he believes "in Providence and the manifest will of the people. . ." and that he "won't be able to run away in the face of the challenge of responsibility."

August. On August 16, President Ch'oe resigns the presidency after a brief vacation. On August 22, Chun Doo Hwan resigns from the Army. On August 27 he is elected President by the National Conference on Unification, the South Korean electoral college.

The "Kwangju Incident" Observed:
An Anthropological Perspective
on Civil Uprisings

Linda Lewis

In the late afternoon of Monday, May 19, 1980 (Day Two of the Kwangju uprising) I made my way from the downtown area of the city, where I had been observing from afar the demonstrations, to my home in a residential section about ten minutes' walk from the Provincial Office Building. I had to go by way of back streets and alleys, avoiding the main thoroughfares, which were blocked off at intersections by lines of soldiers, and were virtually empty of traffic. Most of the shops were shuttered, and the rest were quickly being closed. In contrast, many of the side streets were jammed, back from their entrance onto the main roads, with angry citizens milling about, talking in groups, tense, frightened, upset. The small commercial street nearest my home, when I got to it, was also full. I was told that it had been the scene, not ten minutes before, of a pitched battle between soldiers and citizens, the soldiers driving the townspeople back up the street.

In my field notes for that day I wrote:

> At home, there were three strange high
> school girls who couldn't make it [to their]
> home[s], and are at our place for the night.
> Mother said a grade school kid, along with
> various other citizens, had been killed in the
> [recent street] battle. Hyong Nim ["Big Brother,"
> the college student in the family] reports the
> head of the student body [at Chonnam University]
> is dead. He also got word they [the soldiers]
> are doing house to house searches for students.
> It looks like the soldiers really have the place
> locked up. Mother is really ready to take to the
> streets. This is seen as a conspiracy against

15

> Cholla-do. We are the only ones with a curfew.
> The soldiers are from Kyongsang-do. Also,
> reportedly they're on speed. They are brutal,
> and have been foul of mouth--and singing the
> praises of the late great [President Park Chung
> Hee]. I have also gotten, from several fronts
> including the home front [the Korean family I
> live with]--Why doesn't the US do something?
> Why don't [American] soldiers step in and stop
> this craziness? . . . the worst thing for people
> here is that the rest of the country doesn't know
> what is going on. I called Peterson's [the
> Director of the Fulbright program, in Seoul]--
> no idea anything was happening. Everyone is
> stunned--heartsick.
> . . . It is really horrible, and people can't
> believe it is happening, and can't imagine why."[1]

Why, indeed? Seven years later the question remains unanswered. What sense can be made of the Kwangju uprising? What meaning, or meanings, can be found in it? With the benefit now of some years' hindsight, what is the event's significance, and what implications does it hold?

I bring to this analysis data of a unique kind, gathered in typical anthropological style through participant observation. It was my good fortune (or bad luck, depending on one's perspective) to have chosen Kwangju in 1979-1980 as the site for a research project on the Korean legal system. By May 1980 I was well situated to bear--quite accidentally--anthropological witness to a rebellion.

However, finding a theoretical framework, or disciplinary perspective, within which to understand my material has been more more difficult than I had anticipated. Anthropologists do not usually set out to study civil uprisings. Rather, data gathered in the field is by necessity of the minutiae of daily life, of patterned occurrences. Thus, the anthropologist as serendipidist, observer of the extraordinary, may not find within the discipline analytic models for material unexpectedly obtained. Moreover, the anthropological views of violent protest and rebellion tend, like most work on the subject, toward theories of the longer term, requiring decades of historical context--and usually a clear-cut resolution--to give meaning to specific events. Rebellion is seen as embedded[2] in the context of revolution and social change writ large. It is also, for anthropologists, usually rooted in shifting economic relations in the rural sector.[3] A good deal is known about peasant revolts[4], but little about uprisings in post-peasant societies, about late twentieth century urban insurgency[5], as in the case of Kwangju.

I would like to offer here two approaches to the Kwangju material, two perspectives of the short-run through which to make anthropological sense of the event. The first, a micro-sociological view, pays less attention to broad political context and focuses instead on breaking down the mass of urban rebels into different groups, to distinguish between real populations, and to examine more closely the nature of popular participation in terms of who was involved, to what degree, and with what stakes in the outcome. The other approach looks at the uprising as a violent situation and is concerned with the process of rationalization on the part of the victims. What meanings did people find in the event? What assessments were made by the citizens themselves, and how did they understand, both immediately and in retrospect, the violence that took place?

One of the most important points to be made about the Kwangju uprising is its "popular" nature. It was my observation that participation in the event was city wide and involved a majority of the citizenry. By "participation" I mean the performance at some point in the ten days of a public action demonstrating support for the rebellion, be it[6] appearing at one of the rallies held in the central plaza,[7] giving food or money to the student protestors, engaging in[8] street fighting, or procuring and bearing weapons. I heard no opposition to the rebellion, although some people did choose to leave the city, but more to avoid the appearance of participation, to dissociate themselves from the event, rather than from disagreement with the sentiments of the rebellious populace. I also am aware of no anti- or counter-rebellion incidents, nor does there appear to have been any physical fighting between rival groups of citizens. Reported disagreements between the radical student leadership and the more moderate citizens' committee were over tactical matters, in negotiating with the military, rather than over[9] the fundamental "righteousness" of the rebellion itself. Actually, so widespread was mass support for the uprising that the more interesting question is who did not participate, and why.

Beyond the general engagement of a broad spectrum of the population, three main categories of participants in the uprising can be distinguished on the basis of the nature, extent, and timing of involvement, and stake in the outcome.

There were some groups who were mobilized on the basis of pre-existing ties, and in accord with previously

established (and socially recognized) channels of action and
modes of public protest. These groups by and large were also
involved in active opposition to government policy,
particularly the imposition of martial law prior to May 18,
1980. The most obvious of these were the university students.
Students in Korea have a long tradition of demonstrating
against the government and are recognized as legitimate and
proper leaders of public expressions of political protest.[10]
Other groups in this category were members and leaders of
church and other civic organizations (e.g., the YWCA and
YMCA) active in regular and continuing political opposition.
It was these groups that provided leadership for the
rebellion.[11]

However, the majority of the demonstrators--by far the
largest category numerically and most of the reportedly tens
of thousands who demonstrated in the streets during the
uprising's first days, and most of whom were not armed and
would not have wanted to get hurt--were recruited
individually and were not participating through channels of
previously experienced collective action. Many of these
people were initially engaged in the uprising in the context
of neighborhood street fighting, through either witnessing
some violent incident themselves or hearing a firsthand
account of it. But what is significant about this majority
category--the "masses" of the rebellion--is that they were
not engaged along pre-existing lines, including class
affiliation.

Finally, there were those initially constrained from
acting on the basis of a common vested interest in not being
labelled as participants. In this category are those,
primarily government employees (judges, civil servants,
school administrators--mostly men in positions of public
trust) who were afraid of losing their jobs. It was not that
these people disagreed with the grievances and goals of the
rebellion or that they hoped the rebellion would collapse,
or even that they feared for their lives. Rather as one man,
a teacher, explained to me on May 24,

"Why aren't we going out? says [Mr. X].
Well, it isn't because we are afraid--we aren't,
anymore. In fact, the downtown's safe right now
and stores are open. The problem is that the
authorities (that is, the guys in planes [flying
overhead and dropping leaflets] are telling us to
stay inside. So if we go out, people will see us,
and when this is over, we'll be accused of taking
part."[12]

When the inevitable end to the uprising came and the government regained control, if they were known to have demonstrated, their positions would be in jeopardy. These people were the last to show their support publicly for the uprising.

These categories of participants were engaged in the rebellion in successive stages. The event began as a student demonstration against the imposition of martial law and developed into a series of street demonstrations (in Kwangju, relatively peaceful ones) that were part of an ongoing national pattern of student demonstrations begun in early May. There had been massive demonstrations in Seoul the previous week, and it does not seem that the students in Kwangju were in general doing anything distinctive, compared with students in other cities--except that they agreed to continue demonstrating on May 18.[13]

It should be noted here that, while students were the first participants, not all students participated equally. Many students who demonstrated in the early days went into hiding (often at the behest of their parents) when the violence began.[14] Many of them remained in hiding, even during the least dangerous phases of the rebellion, for fear they, too, would later be singled out as culpable. Ironically, students who demonstrated pre-, but not post-May 18 were replaced on the streets by parents who had earlier counselled caution. One woman, in explaining her concern over her college son's activism, told me on May 14 that "I agree with him that the government is bad. But I urge him not to demonstrate because I worry about him. He could get hurt, or jailed, or thrown out of school.[15] A few days later, this mother was out demonstrating, while her son was confined to the house. It was a relatively small group of students who were active, and armed, participants throughout the whole event.

The situation became an uprising in a second stage, with the subsequent engagement of the largest category, the general citizenry, on May 19, 20, and 21. Initially, and as an explanation of what provoked most of the street fighting in the first days, ordinary people took to the streets as an expression of popular outrage at the brutality of government troops in suppressing the student demonstrations. It was difficult, in fact, to totally avoid involvement in those early days, because so much street fighting went on. People went out to look, and got caught up in it, or went out to join in. There were also a significant number of people who were aware of the brutality and were outraged, but who did not venture far into the streets for fear of getting hurt.

These people, however, participated in other ways (giving food, money) and demonstrated to the extent that it was not, or as soon as it ceased to be, physically dangerous.

This second stage, of engaged mass participation, was followed on May 23 by a third stage, after the troops left the center of the city, when non-violent demonstrations (in the form of mass rallies) numerically reached their peak. And this third stage was distinguished by the emergence of a new grievance, that served to involve the rest of the demonstrators (the category of initially reluctant partici- pants), and which explains what kept people in the streets and strengthened the sense of resistance within the city, prolonging the rebellion. Without this second grievance, the uprising might have collapsed after a couple of days of street fighting. And that grievance was (and still is) that the government refused to apologize or in any way to accept responsibility for provoking the initial violence. A rebellious populace took to the streets as a defensive response to the repressive actions of government troops, and they remained in the streets when the government labelled them hooligans, outlaws and Communists for doing so. And it was at this point, and for this reason, that even civil servants who were putting their jobs at risk began to participate publicly.

Individual rebellions, suggests Elizabeth Perry[16] combine elements of "blind accident and human will". Perhaps what made Kwangju different--in a season of violent urban protest in Korea--was that the blind accident of paratrooper brutality was combined with sufficient human will, in the form of opposition to the implementation of martial law and the return to military rule (and, thus, the turn away from democratic reform). The collapse of the rebellion in the face of the government's armed reentry into the city on May 27 should be viewed not as a sign of a failure of leadership or weakness of popular support so much as a realistic assessment of the lengths to which the government was willing to go in using force to suppress the rebellion. I think we have to see the Kwangju uprising as more than an example of collective violence gone out of control. I would suggest that in fact, at the peak of mass participation, it took on a character not usually associated with rebellions, or, certainly, it attained, in a qualita- tive way, a level of complexity beyond the run-of-the-mill urban riot. And we might question, on a number of grounds, the extent to which it was marked by the "limited stakes," "backward glance," and "low level of ideology"[17] commonly attributed to rebellions. It is especially significant that:

(1) it was not limited to a specific segment of
society, (e.g., urban laborers), but involved a
broad cross-section of the citizenry;

(2) it did not involve the destruction of private
property, and the violence on the part of the
rebels to both person and property was limited to
specific government-related targets;[18]

(3) it possessed a leadership that was, certainly in
terms of the students, part of a national movement
recognized as a force capable of transforming
society; and--while the uprising itself was
sparked by two specific and immediate grievances:
the brutality of the government in suppressing the
demonstrations and the subsequent failure of the
government to accept responsibility for its
actions--the more abstract political goal of the
establishment of a democratic government was
already present.

Turning to a second approach to the Kwangju uprising, I
would like to consider the interpretation of the event's
violence, the process of giving meaning to the violence that
occurred, on the part of the victims--in this case, the
Kwangju citizenry. What sense did people make of it? How did
they seek to justify, explain, or excuse what went on, and
their own part, collective and individual, in it? What
understanding did people have of what they themselves saw or
heard or did? Three primary "meanings," or interpretations,
were expressed again and again during the course of the
uprising.

The first explanation is that the paratroopers who
acted with such apparently random and senseless brutality
during the first three days must have been made crazy--
hopped up, drugged, drunk, denied sleep and starved into
behaving as they did. As my field notes at the beginning
suggest, it was widely reported within the city that the
paratroopers had been specially selected and "prepared" for
their Sunday afternoon appearance in downtown Kwangju. It
was said that their faces were flushed, their breath smelled
of alcohol, and they spoke in Kyongsang-do dialect. A
published account by a Korean journalist reports:

Later I had a chance to talk with a paratrooper who had been captured by the students. I
asked him why they had been so brutal. He told me

that they hadn't been fed for three days, that
immediately before being sent into Kwangju they
had been fed soju (rice wine) [sic] and also
that they had been told they were being sent in
to put down a communist insurrection.[19]

In the apparent outlandishness of these rumors and
allegations about the paratroopers are mirrored the
incomprehensibility of what people saw taking place around
them. The drugged state of the soldiers underscores the
innocence of the victims; that they were starved into
brutality helps explain how they could have been so violent
without any provocation. To the question "What did we do to
deserve this?" the answer, then, is "nothing." And it is
not enough that the paratroopers were reportedly "enemies,"
from the other side of the country, supporters of the former
President and by extension opposed to the political
aspirations of Cholla-namdo's native son, Kim Dae Jung. In
addition, to do such horrible things they must have been
made crazy, been given alcohol, or somehow been put into a
state where they could not have been responsible for their
own actions. Popular interpretation of the events required
the assumption that the perpetrators were not in their
"right" minds. For various reasons, the only meaning to be
found was in the image of drug-crazed troops run amok.

A second "interpretation" I often heard expressed, one
that was articulated in the middle of the uprising and might
have been seen as a justification for armed resistance,
likens the actions of the government to those of the North
Korean communists and/or the Japanese during the colonial
period. It was a judge who I first heard say, "What could
the North Koreans do to us that would be worse than this?" A
May 22 leaflet written by Chosun University students states
that "Older people, seeing this brutal genocide, said that
it was worse than the communists during the Korean War."[20]
And a published eyewitness account, seeking comparison in
the past, says "Today's politicians must awaken from the
mistaken belief left over from the colonial period that
you can overcome any opposition in governing simply by using
force and killing."[21]

I would suggest that this drawing of comparisons with
the actions of Japanese and North Korean occupiers
represented a basic questioning of the legitimacy of the
government's actions. To find analogies, people had to look
to the worst they had (collectively) experienced--Japanese
colonialism, the Korean War--and to the worst they could
imagine--North Korean rule. What kind of government would

respond with such force, against civilians? Both of the examples represent, to South Koreans, governments that obtained and maintained power through violence and repression--and the illegitimate use of force. Participation in the Kwangju uprising, then, particularly in the mass anti-government rallies of May 24-25, was rationalized as a legitimate protest against the illegitimate use of force. It was the government officials, not the citizens of Kwangju, who were the outlaws.

Finally, a last meaning derives from the oft-repeated expectation that the American government would (and should) actively intervene, to stop the armed confrontation. I myself was angered--and puzzled--by the frequently-expressed sentiment that the United States had a responsibility to come to the defense of the city. My notes throughout the period and even for months afterwards make reference to conversations with both friends and strangers about their initial expectations of American support and, later, their surprise and distress at its absence. On May 20 I recorded the following exchange with a close Korean friend who was aware that I was in frequent contact with, David Miller, Director of the local American Cultural Center and the sole American official in Kwangju:

Friend: Miller is a real bastard--he isn't calling Seoul.
Me: But he is.
Friend: No--if he were, the U.S. would do something. [22]

Throughout the uprising, the lack of some overt American action was taken as evidence that the American Embassy in Seoul did not understand what was happening down south, and this idea came from the conviction (to my friends clearly obvious, to me naive, even fantastic) that the U.S. government would step in and stop the violence.

Why would people in Kwangju have expected American intervention? To find the answer, we might look at established patterns for the resolution of conflict in Korean society. One key to explaining violent situations, after all, is an understanding of the more usual, more "normal" non-violent outcomes. What is the Korean conflict scenario, the general procedure by which Koreans approach and deal with contentious situations, and the manner in which disputes are interpreted, carried forward, and resolved?

The nature of conflict in Korean society is relatively unexplored territory, at least by anthropologists, except perhaps for the work of Vincent Brandt, who notes that in a village "the sound and fury of conflict is there for all to see"[23] and who draws our attention to its public nature. As a social process, the Korean culture scenario for conflict resolution involves the public expression of grievances by both sides, as a means of informing the neighbors, of shaping a local consensus, and of mustering popular support for each side in the argument.

It is above all also a process that relies heavily on the involvement of a third, mediating party for a successful outcome. In fact, it is through the public airing of the dispute that the antagonists solicit the intervention of others. Thus, two men stand in the street yelling at each other as a crowd gathers. When the shoving starts, onlookers step forward to restrain the two, reasoning with them and stopping the fight at the point where verbal aggression threatens to erupt into physical violence. In the same manner, an aggrieved landlady and her equally enraged tenant take turns standing in the courtyard, denouncing each other to the world at large in alternating monologues that detail charge and counter-charge. The neighbors listen, and the next day they intervene to prevent the tenant's eviction. Intense verbal aggression and the public expression of grievances serve not as a prelude for physical violence but function to mobilize third party intervention, to prevent just such an escalation of the dispute.

Perhaps it is not possible to project a model for dealing with interpersonal disputes onto collective political action. But, in the context of such a conflict scenario, the expectation of American intervention in the Kwangju uprising gains meaning. Like a daughter-in-law standing on the porch pouring out her grievances into the night, people in Kwangju publicly expressed their side of the story, their sense of having been wronged by the government, expressing it first in the form of defensive armed resistance, then in mass rallies and public demonstrations held in the center of town. And, these citizens were surprised when this failed to elicit intervention on their behalf. Public expression of a dispute is interpreted as a call for intervention; the absence of intervention confounds cultural expectations and leaves the means of the conflict's resolution unclear.

Some final observations can be made about these three "meanings." As historical distance from the Kwangju uprising lengthens and the actual event recedes in time, it is assumed that interpretations of it on the part of the victims are subject to re-evaluation, if only on the basis of the new insights and factual information hindsight may bring. But the Kwangju uprising continues to be invested with these interpretations, now reiterated as the innocence of the victims, the illegitimacy of the government's actions, and the culpability of the United States, through its failure to intervene. And, in fact, from the perspective of those opposed to the present Korean government, these "interpretations" have become the most significant aspects of the Kwangju uprising itself.

NOTES

[1] Personal field notes, May 19, 1980.

[2] The literature on revolutions is voluminous, but as John Walton notes in his work on national revolts, "Based as it is on only a few historical transformations, revolutionary theory avoids the study of major protests that are not historically distant or patterned along classical lines of struggle and resolution. If, for a variety of developmental reasons, modern revolutions present a different complexion and follow a novel path, they are relegated to theoretical limbo—out of bounds for revolutionary theory but within the bounds of no equally rich analytic tradition." Reluctant Rebels (New York: Columbia University Press, 1984), p. 3. See Mark Hagopian, The Phenomenon of Revolution (New York: Dodd, Mead, and Co., 1974), for a discussion of the usual distinctions made between revolutions and other forms of collective protest.

[3] e.g., Eric Wolf, Peasant Wars of the Twentieth Century (New York: Harper and Row, 1969).

[4] See Theda Skocpol, "What Makes Peasants Revolutionary?" Comparative Politics, XIV 14 (1982), pp. 351-375, for a discussion of recent fascination with, and the growing literature on, peasants and revolution.

[5] See Josef Gugler, "The Urban Character of Contemporary Revolutions," Studies in Comparative International Development, XVII, 2 (1982), pp. 60-73.

[6] Refers to the large open area in front of the Provincial Office Building, a central location in downtown Kwangju and the scene of mass anti-government rallies, May 24-26, 1980.

[7]Apparently offering such "logistical" support was widespread. On May 21 a trio of women in my neighborhood collected food door-to-door to give student protestors; I earlier had seen a group of them wrapping rice balls with seaweed and putting in it boxes, also to give to students. On May 26 I was in the local market when the green "paddy wagon" --the van usually used to transport suspects to and from criminal court but now adorned with a paper flower wreath, used as a hearse--pulled up, and out hopped four students. It was a funeral delegation, collecting money for expense. They did not have to solicit contributions. Those in the market mobbed them, waiting in line to push 1,000 won bills into their hands. I estimated they collected 150,000 won (about $250) in five minutes.

[8]See The New York Times, May 22, 1980, which quotes the martial law command as saying that the protestors had more than 3,500 weapons, 46,000 rounds of ammunition, and armored vehicles, and cites estimates of up to 200,000 demonstrators (or 25 percent of the city's population) in the streets.

[9]See Shim Jae Hoon, "Gunfire Ends the Insurrection," Far Eastern Economic Review, May 30, 1980, p. 10, on divisions in the citizens' committee.

[10]See Sungjoo Han, "Student Activism: A Comparison Between the 1960 Uprising and the 1971 Protest Movement," in Chung Lim Kim (ed.), Political Participation in Korea (Santa Barbara, Calif.: Clio Books, 1980), pp. 143-161.

[11]Those Kwangju citizens later detained and charged with responsibility for the uprising included not just students but also priests, professors, lawyers, and YMCA/YWCA leaders. The involvement of some was as members of the citizens' committee, through which they were active in negotiations between the students and the military authorities. See the May 10, 1981 issue of Korea Communique, XXXIX (Tokyo: Japan Emergency Christian Conference on Korean Problems, 1981) for details on those convicted in connection with the uprising.

[12]Personal field notes, May 24, 1980.

[13]See The Asian Wall Street Journal, May 20, 1980, for an account of prior events.

[14] As did many young people who feared being mistaken for college students. So widespread were reports on May 19-20 of random violence by soldiers against young people caught walking downtown that the young male clerks at the district courthouse, for example, were afraid to go near the center of the city.

[15] Personal field notes, May 14, 1980.

[16] Elizabeth Perry, Rebels and Revolutionaries in North China, 1845-1945 (Stanford: Stanford University Press, 1980), p. 252.

[17] Hagopian, p. 12.

[18] Government claims to the contrary, I saw no evidence of looting or vandalism on walks through the downtown area on May 23-26. In contrast, many government buildings-- including all the police stations and boxes I passed and the local tax office--were damaged.

[19] Reports from Kwangju (Washington, D.C.: North American Coalition for Human Rights in Korea, 1980), p. 6.

[20] Ibid., p. 18.

[21] Ibid., p. 15.

[22] Personal field notes, May 20, 1980.

[23] Vincent S. R. Brandt, A Korean Village: Between Farm and Sea (Cambridge: Harvard University Press, 1971), p. 185.

Confrontation in Korean Literature

David R. McCann

> To explain the recurrence [of rebellion] one is
> thus well advised to look carefully at the local
> setting in which it developed.
>
> Local environments are of course a combination of
> natural and social features . . . . The interaction
> between physical and social structures . . . constitutes
> a particular human ecosystem.
>
> Chronic rebellion . . . was a rational extension
> of ongoing modes of resource competition, shaped by the
> natural and social composition of the area.
>
> Elizabeth Perry, <u>Rebels and Revolutionaries in
> North China, 1845-1945</u>.[1]

For a period of several days in May of 1980, the people
of Kwangju, the capital of South Cholla province, demonstrated for open elections, the hope for which had been kindled
in South Korea during the months following the assassination
of President Park Chung Hee in October of 1979. On May 17
as South Korean troops were moving into positions around
Kwangju, martial law was declared.

When demonstrations continued in Kwangju on the following
day, Korean troops moved into the city and began a campaign
of punishment, beating and clubbing the citizens into
submission. The citizens resisted, and eventually drove the
troops out of the city on May 27, despite repeated efforts
by the citizens of Kwangju to engage in negotiations with
the government, Korean troops again invaded the city.

In confronting what happened in Kwangju seven years
ago, the student of literature faces a blank wall. There is

little or nothing that can be called a literary response to the tragedy. The novelist Hwang So-gyong has written a narrative of the Kwangju uprising, entitled <u>Over Death, Over the Darkness of the Age</u> (<u>Chugumul nomo, sidaeui odumul nomo</u>).[2] There are several first-, second-, and third-hand accounts, notably including those published by the North American Coalition for Human Rights in Korea under the title <u>Reports from Kwangju</u>, and a recent paper by Tim Warnberg at the University of Hawaii, "The Kwangju Uprising: An Inside View."[3]. One poem included in the <u>Reports,</u> "O Kwangju! O Mudung Mountain!" is considered near the end of this essay.

Yet the event demands attention, even of the student of literature, who can find few poems, short stories, or novels directly relating to the uprising. <u>Absent</u> the literary works about Kwangju, however, how is one to begin? A book by Elizabeth Perry, quoted in the heading of this essay, provides an adaptable conceptual basis for the attempt. To take Perry at the most literal and simplistic level, does the idea of "ecology"--that is, of large-scale, geographic, climatic, and other, interconnected conditions of life in a particular area--help in any way to explain the Kwangju uprising?

THE POLITICAL ECOLOGY OF THE HONAM REGION

Kwangju, first of all, is geographically isolated. It is a long way from Seoul on a branch of the railroad line, and cut off from neighboring South Kyongsang province by the lower extremities of the extensive and even now relatively unsettled Chiri mountain range. The mountains have had considerable significance historically as a place of refuge for the armies of the Tonghak rebellion in the 1890's; for anti-Japanese guerrillas during the period of the Japanese occupation; and for communist guerillas during the period 1945-1950. This enumeration also will suggest the historical nature of the tradition of rebellion in the southwestern, or Honam region. Such references, comprising part of the Honam regional identity, are illustrated in a poem by Kim Chi-ha,[4] one of a number of well known writers from the region:

Chiri Mountain

When I see
the snow-covered mountain my blood seethes.
When I see the green bamboo groves

my anger blazes.
Beneath those bamboos
below that mountain
even now the crimson blood flowing.
There, far over the plain
the mountain peaks, turning, winding,
flowing into the distance:

A cry
    a banner.
Before burning eyes, the glare of the white
uniforms has vanished.

The rusted scythes, ages-long poverty,
the weeping embrace and the fleeting
promise to return:
all are gone,
yet still cry out in my heart.

Like the current flowing
away under the frozen surface
of the stream
    they have gone,
but like the water's force
even now they return, pounding
voices that will not let me be,
the old songs.

When I see the snow-covered peaks
my blood seethes.
My anger blazes at the sight
of the green groves of bamboo.

                 Even now
living, winding through my heart
is Chiri Mountain.

During the Park Chung Hee regime, the Honam region was
ignored in South Korea's development plans at least in part
because Park's most able political opponent, Kim Dae Jung,
was born there, in the coastal town of Mokp'o.[5] Add to this
the stereotype of the people of Cholla as being backward,
shifty, and slow, a characterization that has been picked up
even in foreign publications about Korea;[6] and add to this
the deployment in the action against Kwangju of troops from
Kyongsang province, a region that has seemed to take special
pride in its contempt for the southwest, and--with the seven

years' hindsight since the event--the outlines of a precarious political situation are disturbingly clear. The Honam region was isolated, economically and politically, and the Korean government made certain that it stayed that way. That situation is even more troubling, given the advanced degree of political polarization of Korea today along the same geographical lines.

What brought the spark to that well-seasoned tinder, transforming demonstrations--which had been occurring elsewhere in Korea for a period of months prior to and after the assassination of Park, Chung Hee--to rebellion, which happened alone in Kwangju?[7] The triggering mechanism for the explosive change from volatile situation to outright rebellion seems to have been nothing other than the sheer brutality of the troops. In Warnberg's account, a student at Chonnam National University related that many of the students "felt they had been forced by the military to defend themselves with arms. . . .`Could we just sit by and do nothing while our neighbors and friends were beaten and killed before our eyes?'" The uprising was not at that point a political movement, ". . .But rather an attempt by the people of Kwangju to defend themselves from what they perceived to be an arbitrary use of military force. That was a theme we heard repeatedly."[8] Ki-baik Lee (Yi Ki-baek) in his New History of Korea notes the same triggering mechanism in the April 1960 Student Revolution against the Syngman Rhee regime:

> After holding a demonstration in front of the National Assembly building, the students headed for Kyongmudae (the presidential residence), . . .only to be met by a hail of police bullets when they reached its vicinity. Roused to a frenzy by the sight of comrades dying before their eyes, the students set fire to a number of government structures and committed other violent acts of destruction.[9]

Reaching a judgment as to the immediate cause of the uprising and the more remote conditions that set the stage for it will require continuing evaluation by historians and other social scientists of the documentary evidence-- evidence which has been impossible to examine in Korea, by government policy. Whether the brutal actions of the troops eventually stand identified as the major immediate cause of the uprising, it is clear that what happened in Kwangju in 1980 was the end product of a long-standing set of conditions in which ecology, as that idea might be loosely adapted from Perry, was a factor.[10]

Hwang So-gyong put these matters as follows:

> A general respite or lull was reached throughout the country, but Kwangju alone was an exception. Instead, some thirty thousand people, even more than on previous days, gathered in front of the provincial administration building with a vast display of blazing torches. After October 26, the strong hope for democratization reached a far higher level in Kwangju than in other regions; and one can point to several reasons for this. First, from the Tonghak farmers' rebellions through the Righteous Armies [of the nineteenth century] through the Kwangju Student Rebellion [of 1929] and other events, there had come into existence a family-like tradition of outstanding pride and self-awareness regarding the democratization movement. Among the proponents of democracy who were then out of power, there were many who had taken leading roles in the Kwangju Student Movement. Members of the younger generation, through the recollections of their families or grandfathers or great-grand-fathers who had been members of the Tonghak, or Righteous Armies, carried in their blood the living vestiges of modern history. Thus in a single family might be found the personification of a full hundred years of modern Korean history.

To be sure, Perry's book described a set of inhospitable ecological conditions that made of the Huai-pei region in China a peripheral area likely to experience the violent forms of peasant adaptation known as rebellions. The issues articulated during the ten days of the Kwangju uprising were social and political, however, rather than a matter of the distribution of scant grain resources. The hostile environment that Kwangju continues to occupy in Korean affairs is political, not meteorological; and the people involved have been urbanites, not peasants.

There are limits, in short, to what an account of the ecology of peasant rebellion in China can tell us about the Kwangju uprising—or Korea in the twentieth century at all. Nevertheless, the idea of an ecological system, and especially of a human ecosystem that may condition certain patterns of behavior, is an intriguing one. How, though, might the idea of a political and social ecosystem be translated into an analytical framework applicable to the study of literature? To try to answer that question is to begin to think about Korean literature in terms that accommodate what happened in Kwangju in 1980.

THE ECOLOGY OF LITERATURE

A language and a literature is a system of signs, one that resembles in significant ways the ecosystem that Perry describes. The relationship of a literary tradition, or a literature, to its given linguistic and cultural setting comprises both natural and social features, and the customary interactions between the physical, linguistic features of language and the social-structural conventions of literature constitute a distinctive literary ecosystem.[11] Just as there can be all manner of human ecosystems, distinguished by such natural variables as the relative availability of resources and of physical access to them; and just as "divisions of class, clan, and settlement shaped the distribution of resources within Huai-pei,"[12] there can be all manner of literary ecosystems as well, similarly shaped by social structures.

In Korea from the earliest written records until the end of the nineteenth century, the language for official communications, and of high literature from histories to essays to poetry, was Chinese. The written language for the common people, for women, and for all non-official, "vernacular" literature, from personal journals to songs, folk tales, and other casual texts, was Korean. Access to the Chinese language and to the system of signs embedded in it was possible only by way of the lengthy training that prepared candidates for the state examinations, and only to the members of the upper class, who could afford it. Access to the Chinese language and literature in Korea was therefore both a means and a signs of access to power. All other language used was peripheral.

The Chinese-Korean symbiosis embedded in the Korean literary ecosystem recalls the dualistic order that Vincent Brandt described in his classic study of the village by the sea--a formal, hierarchical, Confucian central axis about which an informal, egalitarian, vernacular Korean sphere of activity conducted itself.[13] Brandt's study showed how the people of the village moved from one frame of reference to the other, and described the circumstances for the selection of one or the other. In literature, one finds the same dual order of the Chinese and the vernacular Korean traditions.[14] That dualism can be generalized further, and more usefully for twentieth century Korean literature which no longer includes the Chinese, as a relationship between the center and the periphery. Viewed from the center, the periphery is seen as a source and location of disorder, ran.[15] Always under scrutiny and enjoined to stop being disorderly, the periphery views the center with a substantial and well established sense of resentment, or han.[16]

Historically, center and periphery have not always challenged or battled each other, even in matters of serious dispute. In "The Tale of Ch'oyong," for example, from the thirteenth-century compilation of Silla legends and tales known as Samguk Yusa, or Remnants of the Three Kingdoms, the ruler, Hon'gang, is first seen on a picnic in the east, where he encounters the Dragon King of the Eastern Sea. After Hon'gang constructs a shrine and performs the appropriate rites to mark the occasion, the Dragon King introduces his son Ch'oyong into the story and the king's retinue. The story follows Hon'gang on his continuing journeys to the south and to the north, where the rulers fails to discern the message of the spirits that present themselves out on the circuit around the circumference of the capital he is patrolling. Even when a pair of spirits take the quite unprecedented step of appearing before the king at a royal banquet, he foolishly interprets their warning as a good omen and continues with the "revels and debauchery while the kingdom tottered to its fall."[17]

Ch'oyong, whose story occupies the center of the chapter about Hon'gang, is given to similar parties and peregrinations within the capital, away from his home. But unlike the king Ch'oyong knows what to do when he discovers, returning late one night, that the plague demon has assumed human form and has attacked his wife as she lies in her bed. Ch'oyong goes out to the yard of his residence, dances and sings this song:

> Under the moonlight of the capital
> I stayed out on my late night revels.
> Now I return and find in my bed
> four legs.
> Two were once mine,
> but whose are the others?
> Once mine, what shall I do
> Now that they are stolen?[18]

Ch'oyong's song is more diagnosis than complaint: it contains not a word about the people whose legs are referred to, nor the situation that apparently joins them. As the narrative continues, it describes how the plague spirit is shamed into leaving by that display of magnanimity. One can also recognize in Ch'oyong's dance and song a shamanistic rite of exorcism to rid the woman of her illness. The demon is persuaded to leave, then, by the indirection of the performance and diagnosis. The spirit promises not only to leave, but also never to return, even to places that display only a likeness of Ch'oyong. One may infer that the king should have paid equal attention to the spiritual affairs of the kingdom so that, guided by the hints and songs of the spirits he encounters, he could preserve the harmonious order described in the opening of the story, saving it from the disorder and collapse that threaten it at the end.

The nineteenth century <u>Story of Ch'unhyang</u>, a famous, indeed almost emblematically popular Korean folktale and <u>p'ansori</u>* text, bases its plot on the tension between the hierarchical, formal, "Confucian" center and the informal, vernacular periphery. It tells the story of a young woman, Ch'unhyang, the daughter of a <u>kisaeng</u> from the town of Namwon in the same province as Kwangju, who falls in love with the provincial governor's son. The young man is sent back to Seoul to complete his studies and sit for the state examination. During his absence, a new and corrupt governor arrives and tries to make Chu'unhyang his concubine. She refuses him, saying she is already betrothed, at which he has her beaten and imprisoned under a sentence of death.

After a prolonged absence, the hero returns to Namwon as the <u>amhaeng osa</u>, or secret royal inspector. Enroute he happens upon a group of farmers talking and singing, and endeavors to glean from their songs and conversation of the new provincial governor. The news that he hears is not good. Shortly after entering the town of Namwon, he uses a banquet presided over by the new governor as the occasion to compose a warning poem that in effect states the charges against the governor. The warning, a translation into Chinese of the message from the farmers' songs and conversations with the hero, serves to put the governor on notice that the exploitation of the people to support the lavish style of government in Namwon will not be tolerated further:[19]

> Fine wine in golden cups is the common people's blood,
> Viands on jade dishes are the common people's flesh;
> When the grease of the candle drips, the people's tears are falling,

---

*An operatic form of oral narrative.

>The noise of the music is loud, but the people's
>   cries are louder.

The governor and his cohorts are arrested. Ch'unhyang
is reunited with her love, and the blissful couple goes off
to Seoul where they and their descendants live happily.

The contemporary opposition leader Kim Dae Jung
observed in his Prison Writings, that the mere replacement
of the governor at the conclusion of the Ch'unhyang story
did nothing to alleviate the conditions that had permitted
the governor's abuse of power in the first place, and that
the essentially wish-fulfilling ending of the story ". . .
reveal(s) the limits of popular consciousness at that time
as well as the constraints under which these operas were
placed because they were performed in front of aristo-
crats."[20] By the middle decades of the nineteenth century,
however, the same social groups that might have been
beguiled by Ch'unhyang's story were participating in the
rebellions that characterized that century of disorders.[21]

Other examples of a tension--indeed, mutual suspicion--
between center and periphery are to be found in the sijo and
kasa poetry of the Yi period, in the songs said to have been
written by court officials being sent into exile or to their
deaths, or challenged to consider the possibility of it. One
of the most widely known examples is by the scholar-official
Chong Mong-ju (1337-1392), who was challenged at a banquet
during the last days of the Koryo Dynasty to consider
shifting his allegiance to the rising faction of General Yi
Song-gye. The challenge took the form of a sijo--by the
fifth son of T'aejo, founder of the Yi dynasty--celebrating
the carefree life of those who could accommodate themselves
to change:[22]

>What does it matter
>   if you do this or that?
>Who cares if the arrow-roots
>   go entangled on Mansu Hill?
>We could be like those vines,
>   enjoying ourselves for a hundred years.

Bravely eschewing metaphor, Chong is said to have
replied with the following:[23]

>Though this frame should die and die,
>   though I die a hundred times,
>My bleached bones all turn to dust,
>   my very soul exist or not--

What can change the undivided heart
the glows with faith toward my lord?

The members of the Yi faction understood Chong's poem
well enough, and assassinated him. Whatever the truth of the
story, Chong's sijo has become the best-known example of the
genre, perhaps as much for its bold rhetoric as for whatever
literary qualities can be identified in so brief a text.

The tension assumes a certain conventionalized
poignance in the kisaeng sijo in which the woman looks back
to the capital, to the center, or nim kyesinun kot or
lover's dwelling-place, to which the lover has returned
after a period of time spent in rusticity. A typical
example is a song by the kisaeng Maehwa:[24]

Were I to draw from my heart
its turmoil, thread by thread,
and weave your abiding place
on the moon-bright bedroom curtains,
then you might know
how deep is my longing.

Center and periphery face one another in the satire of
the puppet plays and mask dance dramas, where the clever
commoners have their rowdy fun at the expense of the foolish
yangban and lascivious monks who attempt to prop up their
questionable dignity with long, nonsensical (Chinese)
passages from Confucian or Buddhist texts. A representative
example, from the Hahoe Mask Dance, finds the scholar
(Sonbi) and the aristocrat (Yangban) arguing over lineage:[25]

Yangban: (Suddenly angry at Sonbi): How dare you act
         in such a way in front of me!
Sonbi: How on earth can you behave that way
         towards me?
Yangban: Well. So, do you mean your lineage is as noble
         as mine?
Sonbi: Does it mean your family is superior to mine?
[Imae and Chorengi imitate their masters' exaggerated
         displays of power in pantomine.]
Yangban: Of course my lineage is superior to yours.
Sonbi: Why is that so? Explain it to me.
Yangban: I'm a descendant of a sa-taebu.*

---

*A Sa-taebu is a person of high rank. Sa can also mean
"four."

Sonbi: What? <u>Sa-taebu</u>? I'm a descendant of a
         <u>p'al-taebu</u>.
Yangban: What on earth is a p'al-taebu?
Sonbi: <u>P'al-taebu</u> is twice the size of a <u>sa-taebu.</u>

And so they continue for the remainder of the play.

In the twentieth century, Korea found itself under Japanese rule (1910-1945), and in such poems as Yi Sang-hwa's "Does Spring Return to Stolen Fields?" one finds a strong echo of the Song of Ch'oyong, both in the form and the content of the ceremony designed to confront the occupying force. Like Ch'oyong, the speaker in Yi's poem goes out into the country- side and performs a dance-like incantation to drive out the Japanese spirits that had stolen--using the word <u>ppaeda</u> for the deed, precisely the same as in Ch'oyong's song--the Korean fields. The first and concluding sections of the poem are as follows: [26]

Does Spring Return to Stolen Fields?

Now another's land--
Will spring return again to stolen fields?
My body moves through sunlight
as I walk and walk the path
parting a dream
between sky and earth.
My soul, like a child
emerging by the river
running free, unbounded:
What is it you are seeking?
Where do you soar?

Along the verge between new joy
and newer sorrow ,
I walked the whole day, to return lame.
I have sensed the spirit of spring,
but these fields are stolen,
and the spring itself
may be stolen.

Notably absent from the poem is any expression of malice, while immanent throughout is the Korean land itself

---

*<u>P'al</u> is a homonym for "eight." "P'al-taebu"--if there were such a thing--might thus be a pun suggesting that Sonbi is twice as high in rank as Yangban.

in the role of a witness or audience to the complaint of the poem. It would seem that theft, as in the Japanese occupation of Korea or the demon's attack on Ch'oyong's wife, is an easier dispute to resolve. Ownership, loss, and the return of something or someone, in other words, seems to be more easily resolved, at least in the literary examples, than conflicts about abstract principles. The argument between Ch'unhyang and the governor, concerned with principles of loyalty and chastity, was resolved only by the exercise of the governor's greater power, in the first instance, when he had her jailed; and by the secret inspector's preeminent power over local administrators.

Two poems by one of Korea's foremost twentieth century writers, So Chong-ju, describe how confrontation leads to violence. The two are taken from So's recently published verse autobiography, <u>Unforgettable Things</u>:[27]

April Revolution

Master A and Master C,
two young poet students
at K High School
were visiting my home
in the time just before
the April Revolution.
A few days before the nineteenth,
Master C appeared alone one day
and told me
the following:

"They were saying
things had gone crazy
down by City Hall,
and the two of us,
A and I,
went down to see.
But when the shooting started
Bang and Bang in all directions
we grabbed hands
the two of us
and ran like mad.
But A was hit
by a bullet
and died and
I was left
all alone
alive."

Masters A and C are the perennial bystanders. They hear about the commotion of April 1960, and go down to see for themselves. The police rifles, perhaps in that hail of bullets cited in Ki-baik Lee's New History, kill Master A.

The two student poets were motivated by nothing more than the same youthful curiosity that had led So Chong-ju and some of this classmates, in an earlier poem recounting his own school days, to run away from class and watch a funeral procession passing the school. The poem about the April Revolution left Master C alive, alone, perhaps in the next year to go off to the university, where the experience recounted in the poem may have propelled him into some kind of student leadership in the following year's demonstrations. The poem left unspoken the grief of A's parents. The poet was left to tell the story of the two otherwise anonymous students.

Kwangju Student Incident

A day in November, 1929,
when the Kwangju student demonstrations
caught fire in Seoul too.
Just thirteen, I
followed out of curiosity
the upperclassmen who led,
shouting "Long live Korean independence!"
As we reached the headquarters
for the Japanese Governor-General, mounted
police drove us like sheep into a corner.
From the police station yard,
one by one we were dragged into a room,
stripped to the waist,
beaten fifteen, twenty times
with leather straps.
Those who had been followers
were turned loose,
though for days after I could not lie down
in bed, for the soreness.
Each day angrier, I muttered at them
"Butcher's bastards! Just you wait!"

This episode from 1929, also from the book
Unforgettable Things,28 bears an unmistakable likeness to
the story of Master A and Master C, at least in the
beginning section. In the poem describing the 1929 incident,
the students directed their procession toward the Japanese
Government-General headquarters, while in the poem about the

1960 revolution the students marched toward City Hall. In both instances, it would appear that the leaders were quite unknown to most of those who participated, and further, that the first stage of participation was motivated more by curiosity than any strong sense of political commitment.

So Chong-ju has two other poems about the Kwangju incident, however.[29] In the second, he has become one of the leaders, and is taken before the public prosecutor. In the third, having transferred to another school, he is placed under police surveillance, and eventually advised to withdraw from school in order to avoid permanent expulsion. The sequence of poems about the Kwangju Student Rebellion of 1929 thus marks out the point of progression in an individual's life from youthful curiosity to political activism.

In reading So Chong-ju's poems, one may discern several of the elements and relationships contained in the literary ecosystem we have been describing. The center in the poems is symbolized by the government buildings towards which the student demonstrators make their way. The periphery is again defined, by elimination, as everything else--up as close to the gates of Kyongmudae as the government troops and police will allow the demonstrators to approach. The young student and his companions are left standing on the near periphery, therefore, in a position that could appear threatening to those who occupy the center.

This state of psychic siege is rendered with a remarkably clear eye in Kim Chi-ha's poems. In the beginning of one, "By the Sea," he summarizes in the first few lines the entire process of inner exile that he was forced to endure in the late 1970's:[30]

> Snow is falling.
> I drink cheap whiskey
> and chew the tears
> that fall on the dried fish
> I chew the sighs
> within my fearful heart, my gestures,
> and each path I have in secret come down
> I am alone.
> In this last space, an edge
> too small for a pin,
> I am alone,
> my friends.

At the time of the poem's composition, Kim Chi-ha was in fact in exile, secluded in the southwestern part of the

42

country near his hometown in Cholla province. The poem can be read as a straightforward description of the poet's own situation, but it also represents the situation of anyone in Korea whose political opinions were not to the government's liking. Kim presents a similar account of Korea--that is, of a land of vast distance between the center of power and authority and the figurative space that any one person occupies--in a brief poem about imprisonment:[31]

Two A.M.

2:00 A.M. is the middle hour.
Unable to sleep, to splash my face with cold water,
to read a book.
Too exhausted to do any writing;
not enough room to get up and walk.

Eating a crust, I feel sorry for my neighbors;
muttering something, embarrassed
at myself. Unable just to sit still.
Unable to do anything.
2:00 A.M
The middle hour,
this age.

The poem is all the more effective because it never refers explicitly to prison, but leaves the reader to conclude that if it is about prison, it is also about Korea, and vice versa.

Kim Chi-ha most strongly expresses the confrontation between center and periphery in a poem called, aptly enough, "Seoul." The poet identifies Seoul as the center and locus of power, a power symbolically so complete that nothing can prevail against it. The final stanza of the poem describes the ultimate, desperate gesture of the individual on the periphery confronting the monolith standing at the center:[32]

Seoul

Where a sword stands,
fog-shrouded, its blade
invisible. Where all traces
of blood flowing through the night
are hidden. Where the fog-shrouded
sword stands deep blue, dark
in   daylight.

Swamp, accursed capital:
your skies are filled where that sword stands.
At last to defeat you,
to defeat you, Seoul,
I have offered up my life
with no part of it kept back
to your blade.

Even my starving, sick depleted body
burning away in undeterred revolt.
At the end
it remains as something to strike with
down onto the blade
onto the blade of the sword
like the flower's red, red falling
to defeat you;
to die and at last defeat you.
To die
that in my blood your blade
rust away.

CONFRONTATION, VIOLENCE, AND REPRESSION

Some movements arise primarily because of
perceived <u>political</u> deprivation; that is, the
group involved in the action believes that it is
not possible to act effectively through the usual
political channels, even though socially and
economically they do not see themselves as being in
a deprived situation.[33]

"Agh! What a dog's life this is!"
(The character Ando in the poem "The Story of a
Sound," from the sequence of three poems,
<u>Groundless Rumors,</u> by Kim Chi-ha.)[34]

From Ch'oyong to Chong Mong-ju, from Ch'unhyang to So
Chong-ju, Kim Chi-ha, and other contemporary writers, the
moment and the act of confrontation are a characteristic of
Korean literature. In The Story of Ch'oyong and other
stories recorded in the <u>Samguk Yusa</u>, the spirits or other
antagonists respond to human entreaties by repenting and
restoring what they had taken. Once into the Yi Dynasty, the
powers-that-be were not so kind. The response to Chong
Mong-ju's famous <u>sijo</u> about his steadfast loyalty was his
death at the hand of a government assassin. In the story of

Ch'unhyang, the heroine's elaborate, Confucianist plea serves only to enrage further the corrupt governor, who is quite prepared by the end of the tale to have her executed for her continued defiance.

The _sijo_ by officials and _kisaeng_ both, convey or embody the implicit wish that the other, the one spoken to or about, will hear the song and be moved to relent. _Sijo_ songs are a form of conventionalized or stylized reproach. They threaten nothing, and their appeal is a most gentle one. In this century during the Japanese occupation. Yi Sang-hwa's poem sounded a distant echo of Ch'oyong's in its demonstration against Japan. These songs and poems would coax the source and cause of the affliction, whether it be disease or emotional pain, out into the open. Such stylized confrontation in literature finds its counterpart in political confrontation, where demonstrations accompanied by printed or painted signs, chanting, and the processional choreography of the march, serve to coax the oppressor out into the open. Once drawn into direct confrontation, the source of the affliction must in turn act, either acceding to the demands, or attempting to force those who are demonstrating to stop.

In the twentieth century, Korean political protests have come to be mounted on an international stage, though not always with the hoped-for result of foreign inter-vention, or at least condemnation of the precipitating condition. A Korean mission to the Hague Conference in 1907 to protest the rapidly tightening Japanese hold on Korea served only to provoke the Japanese into forcing King Kojong's abdication. In 1919, following the publication of Wilson's Fourteen Points, Korean protests against continued Japanese rule broke out in many of the major cities and smaller towns as well. Seeing no sign of European or American sympathy for the Korean Independence movement, however, the Japanese simply crushed it. In 1960, Syngman Rhee had been willing enough to order the same fate for the student protestors, but the army refused to carry out his commands, and the United States government managed to let it be known that Rhee had lost its confidence. Fortunately, Rhee resigned. After narrowly losing to Park Chung Hee in the 1971 presidential elections in Korea, Park's opponent, Kim Dae Jung, was kidnapped from a hotel in Tokyo and nearly murdered by the Korean C.I.A. Quick and forceful Japanese and American protests were a factor in preventing the Korean government from having Kim Dae Jung killed.

With Kim Chi-ha in the 1960's and 1970's, one finds the life and the literary works brought forcefully together as a symbol of protest and direct confrontation with Park. In its effort to silence the poet, the Korean government resorted to repeated arrests, trials, and imprisonments. Again, foreign protests and indignation helped deter the government from carrying out the death sentence it imposed against him.

The demonstrations in 1980 had the effect, certainly, of provoking the government into direct confrontation with the people of Kwangju, and the government, just as certainly, did not hesitate to pursue the violent attacks that comprised one of several possible responses. The symbolism of certain key elements in that confrontation is strongly apparent. When the troops first went into the city, they began immediately to use their long clubs to attack the citizens—for the most part at first, the male citizens. The clubs maim and punish; they symbolize the government's powers of chastisement. Similarly, the ferocity of the attack on the buildings housing the radio stations suggests the powerful symbolic importance of those buildings. The perceptions by the outside world, Korean and international, of what was occurring within the city were mediated by the press—far more noticeably so, given first the geographic isolation and then the military blockade of the city, than under more normal circumstances. Awareness of or belief in that external attention appears to be a critical element in preventing confrontation from collapsing into violence. In more normal times, men do shout angrily at one another in a street-side disputes, raising their fists and advancing upon one another in elaborate shows of violent threat, all the while looking around to make sure that someone else is there to hold them back, to contain the violence as a referee does at a boxing match. Should there be no external observer, or one or both parties to the dispute believe there is none, the confrontation is far more likely to become violent.

CONCLUSION

One is left to wonder at the appalling violence of the Kwangju uprising. "Rebellion" is too chaste a term for what happened, and incorrectly implies that the citizens were the sole instigators of what took place. "Uprising" is even less satisfactory, suggesting little more than a low hill on some distant landscape rather than troops clubbing and bayoneting people in the streets, alleys, and houses of a city. That violence is of a piece with the sexual torture of a woman prisoner in Korea in the summer of 1986'[35] and the torture death early in 1987 of a student prisoner that continues to be a rallying point for demonstrations in Korea against the present regime.

The Korean government naturally wishes to ignore Kwangju, or to diminish its significance. Government estimates of the deaths during the uprising remain absurdly low; the motives for the uprising are assigned to "impure elements;" and the contagion of the rebellion is said to have been spread by "groundless rumors," the government's phrase for accounts that differ from its own. The government's account, in fact, amounts to little more than the script for a melodrama, filled with an array of stock characters, from kindly but harried government troops, to innocent citizens, outside agitators, North Korean agents, hoodlums, and the perennial scapegoat in government accounts of domestic disturbances, the students.

What happened in Kwangju follows a pattern that is characteristic in Korean history, of the battle between center and periphery. This paper has endeavored first to characterize the structure of that confrontation, and second, to observe its reflection in examples of Korean literature taken from several disparate points in Korean history. This examination of confrontation in Korean literature began with the observation that the Kwangju incident has not yet appeared in contemporary Korean literature. It may be too much to ask of literature; or rather, Kwangju may still to too directly disturbing an incident to the world of literature. The novelist Hwang So-gyong's account, documentary in intent, is nevertheless a powerful narrative of those days in 1980. The one poem to have emerged from the uprising, "O Kwangju, O Mudung Mountain," was written by Kim Chun-tae, a teacher at a high school in Kwangju. The poem speaks in a number of voices-- from a distant point of observation, in the collective voice of the citizens of Kwangju, to the lamenting voice of those who died. But it depends for its overall structural support and symbolic reference upon the image of the risen Christ, and it finds solace, for all the horror of the event, in a conclusion that recalls specifically the Resurrection in an exclamation of faith as strong as it is desperate:[36]

> Bearing the cross of this land
> Returning over Golgotha,
> Son of our nation's god:
> Jesus who once died
> and rose again:
> Has He not lived until today,
> and forever?

And we who have died by the hundreds,
our true love will return to life.
Our fire! Our glory! Our pain!
Even more surely, we shall survive.
Our strength increases, and even we
shall rise into the blue heavens
and touch our lips to the sun and moon.
O Kwangju! O Mudung Mountain!
Our eternal banner,
dream,
and cross.
Even as life flows on,
City of Youth
may you be ever younger.
For now we are sure,
gathering together. Hands joined
in sure affirmation,
we have risen.

There are many precedents for the events in Kwangju,
and many signs throughout Korean history of the confrontation between center and periphery. While that confrontation
is an archetype in modern political poems as well as in
earlier, vernacular, popular expressions of hostility or
amusement at the symbols of power and authority, it has not
yielded a form or subject matter sufficient to express it.
That is, the world of literature seems no more able at this
moment than the government to provide an account of what
happened.[37] That confrontation, between the government's
wish to have the events of 1980 forgotten and the increasing
insistence of the people of Korea that they be openly
addressed and given some meaning, must ultimately yield
itself up to some accounting. The continuing existence of a
group of writers who have named themselves after the event,
as the May 18 Group, is but one sign of the determination of
today's poets and novelists to find a way at some point in
their work to deal with the Kwangju uprising. The government
is likely to find those works offensive, or seditious; it
may label them "groundless rumors," and decide to punish the
writers and publishers and readers for propagating them.
But if the history of Korean literature is any example, and
particularly if writers like Kim Chi-ha and Hwang So-gyong
take up the task, their works will continue to map out the
process of politicization that Korean society and culture
have been subject to. They may also serve to remind those of
us who live in a culture that has trivialized poetry and
made entertainers of poets that the literary act was once a

48

serious and meaningful one. It remains a serious one in Korea, with consequences as unpredictable as those for going off to college or the university, or on certain days, as in Kwangju on a Sunday in May, 1980, for a walk downtown.

NOTES

[1] Elizabeth J. Perry, <u>Rebels and Revolutionaries in North China, 1845-1945</u> (Stanford, Calif.: Stanford University Press, 1980), p. 249.

[2] Hwang So-gyong, <u>Chugumul nomo, sidaeui odumul nomo</u> (Over Death, Over the Darkness of the Age) (Washington, D.C.: The Capital Union Presbyterian Church for Koreans, 1985).

[3] North American Coalition for Human Rights in Korea, <u>Reports from Kwangju</u> (Washington, D.C., 1980); and Tim Warnberg, "The Kwangju Uprising: an Inside View," forthcoming in <u>Korean Studies</u> vol. XI (1987).

[4] Kim Chi-ha, <u>The Middle Hour: Selected Poems of Kim Chi Ha</u> (Stanfordville, New York: Human Rights Publishing Group, 1980), p. 51.

[5] Nena Vreeland et al., <u>Area Handbook for South Korea</u> American University Foreign Area Studies Series (Washington, D.C.: U.S. Government Printing Office, 1975), pp. 180-181.

[6] Patricia M. Bartz, <u>South Korea</u> (Oxford: Clarendon Press, 1972), p. 181.

[7] On the difficulty of accounting for the outbreak of violence at political demonstrations, see Herbert M. Kritzen, "A Theory of Unconventional Political Action: the dynamics of confrontation," in Marjo Hoefnagels (ed.), <u>Repression and Repressive Violence</u> (Amsterdam: Swets and Zeiflinger, 1977), pp. 121-130.

[8] Warnberg, pp. 19-20.

[9] Ki-baik Lee, <u>A New History of Korea</u> (Cambridge, Mass.: Harvard University Press, 1984), pp. 384-385.

[10] Hwang, p. 19.

[11] For an extensive discussion of the relations between natural and social features of verse literature, see Craig La Driere, "Prosody," in Alex Preminger (ed.), Encyclopedia of Poetry and Politics (Princeton, New Jersey: Princeton University Press, 1965), pp. 669-677. Note especially page 670: "Prosodic structures differ from language to language, for twenty-two languages differ in their selection and emphasis among universally available phonetic elements and modes of combining them . . . ;" and page 677: "The selection of elements for metrical schematization and of types of schemes is determined in part by the nature of a language, in part by historical accident. . . ."

[12] Perry, p. 250.

[13] Vincent S.R. Brandt, A Korean Village: Between Farm and Sea (Cambridge, Mass.: Harvard University Press, 1971), pp. 25-29 et passim.

[14] See, for example, David R. McCann, "Formal and Informal Korean Society: A Reading of Kisaeng Songs," in Laurel Kendall and Mark Peterson (eds.), Korean Women, View from the Inner Room (New Haven, Connecticut: East Rock Press, 1983, pp. 129-137.

[15] Ran, or nan, a term of ubiquitous reference in Korea, means disorder or confusion, and by extension, "a war; a rebellion; a revolt; an insurrection; a riot; a disturbance." The New World Comprehensive Korean-English Dictionary (Seoul: Si-sa-yong-o-sa, 1985), p. 412. The word is commonly attached to a date or an agent. Thus, the Japanese invasions of 1592 are known for the cyclical year and agent as Imjin waeran, or the Japanese (wae) disturbance (ran) of the cyclical year "Imjin" (1592). The Tonghak and Righteous Army rebellions of the 1890's are also known as ran: Tonghangnan, and uibyongnan.

[16] Han, translated variously as "a bitter feeling; a grudge; . . . resentment; rancor; . . . regret . . ." in The New World Comprehensive Korean-English Dictionary, p. 2332, is as pervasive and representative a term as ran. In literature it shades off into the poignant laments of the sijo at one end of its spectrum of meanings; it is found at the other extreme, among other places, in Kim Chi-ha's poems of bitter protest from the 1970's.

50

[17] Ilyon, <u>Samguk Yusa: Legends and History of the Three Kingdoms of Ancient Korea</u> (Seoul: Yonsei University Press, 1972), p. 128.

[18] Translated by David R. McCann.

[19] Chong-un Kim and Richard Rutt (trans.), <u>Virtuous Women: Three Masterpieces of Traditional Korean Fiction</u> (Seoul: Korean National Commission for UNESCO, 1974), p. 330.

[20] Kim Dae Jung, <u>Prison Writings</u> (Berkeley, California: University of California Press, 1987), p. 153.

[21] See Ki-baik Lee, pp. 254-255.

[22] Jaihiun Joyce Kim (trans. and ed.), <u>Master Sijo Poems from Korea</u> (Seoul: Si-sa-yong-o-sa, 1982), p. 25.

[23] Richard Rutt, <u>The Bamboo Grove: An Introduction to Sijo</u> (Berkeley, California: University of California Press, 1971), poem 56.

[24] David R. McCann (ed.), <u>Black Crane: An Anthology of Korean Literature</u>, Cornell University East Asia Papers No. 14, 3d printing (Ithaca, New York: Cornell China-Japan Program, 1987), p. 59.

[25] Oh Kon Cho (trans.), "The Hahoe Mask Dance," in McCann (ed.), <u>Black Crane</u>, pp. 51-52.

[26] McCann, "Introduction," in McCann (ed.), <u>Black Crane</u>, p. 6.

[27] So Chong-ju, <u>Unforgettable Things</u> (Seoul: Si-sa-yong-o-sa, 1987), p. 122.

[28] So Chong-ju, p. 35.

[29] So Chong-ju, pp. 37, 39.

[30] Kim Chi-ha, p. 69.

[31] Kim Chi-ha, p. 67.

[32] Kim Chi-ha, p. 73.

[33] Kritzen, in Hoefnagels (ed.), pp. 111-112.

[34] Kim Chi-ha, p. 38.

[35] The case is described in Korea/Update No. 80 (August 1986), published by the North American Coalition for Human Rights in Korea. See "Document from Korea: A Bill of Indictment," pp. 3-9.

[36] Reports from Kwangju, pp. 22-23 (under the title "Kwangju, Cross of our Nation").

[37] Metaphor is insufficient for such pain; thus the poem ends with the Resurrection. See Elaine Scarry, "The Inexpressibility of Physical Pain," in The Body in Pain, The Making and Unmaking of the World (New York: Oxford University Press, 1985) pp. 3-11 and passim. Poetry is insufficient for the rage in Kim Chi-ha's "Seoul;" thus the apocalyptic solipsism of the last ten lines.

Americans and
the Kwangju Incident:
Problems in the Writing of History

Mark Peterson

The Kwangju Uprising poses an interesting set of problems for the historian whose duty it is to write a dispassionate, complete and accurate account of events. In the case of Kwangju, many accounts are passionate, partial and inaccurate. Most of the problems are centered in the fact that the event is so recent; indeed, in the view of many the event is not yet over--it is unresolved. Questions involving the legitimacy or illegitimacy of the government, the unrepentant attitude of the army, and the unforgiving citizens of Kwangju are all unresolved. And the information is similarly problematic. The official account is widely at variance with eyewitness accounts. Newspapers and periodicals contain important elements of the public record but leave other questions unanswered. One advantage to the historian in writing recent history, however, is that some of the participants are willing to respond to the interviewer's questions. This paper is based on official and eyewitness accounts, the public record, and recent interviews with the two ranking American officials in Korea at the time, Ambassador William H. Gleysteen and General John A. Wickham.

Before I present the various accounts of the uprising and examine the available sources, I should provide a basic outline of what happened. It is important to place Kwangju in its historical perspective. The narrative should begin with the assassination of President Park Chung Hee on October 26, 1979, which paved the way for a military coup by Major General Chun Doo Hwan on December 12, 1979. In that coup, initially of limited scope, General Chun and a handful of his colleagues, all classmates from the eleventh class of the Korean Military Academy (1955), seized control of the military. Gradually, under martial law the military extended its control into every sector of society, initially using the excuse of cleaning up or purifying society. While professing their intention to return to the barracks, the military gradually grew in influence between December 12 and early May. Chun's personal power grew as well. By the middle of April, when he assumed the directorship of the Korean Central Intelligence Agency (KCIA), few had any doubts left that Chun had political ambitions. (The U.S. officially and publicly criticized the action.) Certain civilian elements, fearing what had been thought unthinkable for a country now "much too sophisticated for a military takeover," began to mobilize and push for the lifting of martial law.

The student demonstrations spilled off the campuses and into the streets, building to a crescendo on May 15. Meanwhile, professors, religious leaders and writers signed petitions calling for and end to martial law. Members of the National Assembly declared that on the following Monday, May 19, they were going to pass a resolution calling for the lifting of the martial law decree.

Friday, May 16, the nineteenth anniversary of the 1961 military coup, was a remarkably calm day. Student leaders, fearing manipulation by the military and suspicious of agents provocateurs, called off all demonstrations. On Saturday, May 17, the first indications of the military's intentions were revealed when the army raided the Ewha University campus to break up a meeting of student leaders debating future actions. Among the students were those who believed that they had the government on its heels and argued that they should press forward with larger demonstrations. But there were others who argued that the army had as yet-untapped powers to unleash on society and a more cautious approach was warranted. The latter view turned out to be correct, but alas, it was already too late. Soldiers broke into the meeting and arrested all but a few--the few who managed to jump out windows and escape. (My source on the details of the student meeting was one of those who got away that day and went into hiding for several months.)

Later that night, the three Kims--Kim Dae Jung, Kim Young-sam and Kim Chong-p'il--were arrested and an expanded version of martial law was extended throughout the country. The clamping down on demonstrators in Seoul was effective. Special Forces "Black Beret" units, their men identified by black belts, were stationed on major campuses while regular army units set up bivouac on smaller campuses. Tents were pitched conspicuously on athletic fields and soldiers rotated on and off duty at all campus gates, controlling access.

The tactics were as large a failure in the city of Kwangju, however, as they were a success elsewhere in Korea. In Kwangju the demonstrations had already spilled out of the campus and were centered on the main street downtown in the area near the Provincial Capitol Building, the toch'ong. When the military realized that they were already one step behind, having failed to contain the demonstrations on the campus, they resorted to more drastic measures than those being used by their counterparts in Seoul. At about 3:00 p.m. on Sunday, May 18, the Black Berets began breaking into small squads and roaming the downtown streets clubbing and rifle-butting groups of demonstrators and groups that looked like they might be demonstrators. The demonstrators fled for safety into nearby buildings. The Black Berets entered buildings and clubbed and beat any young person there, whether or not they had seen the young person in the streets demonstrating. Their indiscriminate brutality enraged an already indignant core of students and, more important, ordinary citizens, so that demonstrations continued the next day.

On Monday the Black Berets, having found themselves unsuccessful at putting down the demonstrations, escalated the level of violence and tried to terrorize the students and other citizens into clearing the streets. On Tuesday, the violence increased even more. At some point, the Black Berets alienated the local police force and many policemen began to cooperate with the citizens in their battle against the rapacious special forces. Police boxes and their arms caches were opened to the citizenry.

The critical battle came on Wednesday, when the citizens forced the Black Berets to retreat from the city entirely. The key action was the assault on the toch'ong, the bastion of the Black Berets. It was led by taxi drivers, who had met on an athletic field at the opposite end of town to plan a response to the brutality suffered by some of their number who had been beaten for helping carry bloodied and injured citizens to local hospitals, the primary one being located behind the toch'ong. Several taxi drivers had been beaten or killed when trying to carry wounded to the hospital. After meeting and planning their assault, the drivers drove columns of taxis down Kumnam Street and broke through the defenses around the toch'ong, scattering the Black Berets and forcing them to retreat to the edge of the city. The troops were thus defeated by the organized efforts of unarmed civilians.

For the next week, until early in the morning of Tuesday, May 27, the citizens organized various committees for negotiations with the army and management of affairs inside the city, which was effectively cordoned off from the outside world. Contrary to government reports, the situation could not be described as lawless. The impromptu organizations and the spirit of cooperation within the city were remarkable. Some people hoped for a mediated settlement, while others feared that eventually troops would reinvade the city. Eventually, the Twentieth Division of the R.O.K. regular army was released from duties in the Seoul area and sent into the city the the pre-dawn light of Tuesday morning. Only a few still were holding out at the toch'ong when the assault took place; those who died numbered around thirty. With the fall of the toch'ong, the center point of the resistance, the army was able to move throughout the city and reestablish martial law. The uprising was over.

The official account provided by the Korean government at the time was that the citizens of Kwangju were instigated to riot by "impure elements," a term used to mean either North Korean agents or North Korean sympathizers in the South. In particular, Kim Dae Jung, who had been arrested early in the morning of May 18, was charged with inciting the resistance the began after he was taken into custody.[1] The official account has its problems. Indeed, in the early days of the uprising the government's account that four soldiers and only one civilian had been killed (when indeed many had died) infuriated the citizenry to the extent that they burned the building housing the Munhwa Broadcasting Company that had broadcast the story. The MBC building, along with the tax office and the labor ministry office, were the only major buildings destroyed during the uprising.

Eyewitness accounts varied greatly. The point of contention in the abovementioned MBC case, the number dead, continues to this day to be unresolved. The government states that around two hundred died, while others claim a number closer to two thousand. One of the better and more reasonable eyewitness accounts has been written by Tim Warnberg, then a Peace Corps Volunteer and now a graduate student at the University of Hawaii. (His account appears in volume XI of the journal Korean Studies, published by the Center for Korean Studies at the University of Hawaii.) Warnberg handles the body-count controversy by stating that even one death was too many. While he has a point, and Ambassador Gleysteen tends to agree, one cannot help but feel that in Korean society, where ceremonies for the dead are so important and where martyrs such as those killed on April 19, 1960, are honored in a special cemetery, the Kwangju incident will not be over until the dead can be properly honored. That means more than merely accounting for the number killed. It is supposed that many of the bereaved are hiding the fact that a son or daughter or other family member is dead for fear of government reprisals. One aspect of the many eyewitness accounts involved questions of U.S. involvement. Several eyewitnesses noted that the military equipment used by the Korean army was supplied by the U.S. The State Department has repeatedly denied involvement or even knowledge of the Black Berets' actions, but has admitted allowing the Twentieth Division to be released from the US-ROK Combined Forces Command in order to retake the city.

The role of the American government and its representatives in Korea has been severely criticized, but those representatives, Ambassador William Gleysteen and General John Wickham, have recently started to tell their side of the story. Gleysteen has written an account in which he tells his side of the story and some of the insider details concerning four major events in Korea during the time he was ambassador.[2]

Early in 1987, both Ambassador Gleysteen and General Wickham agreed to discuss events surrounding the Kwangju incident with me in what turned out to be insightful interviews. I felt that it was especially significant that a sitting Army Chief of Staff would allow himself to be interviewed concerning his past activities. Both men were candid and anxious to correct certain aspects of the public record. Both spoke of the so-called "myths" that have grown up after the Kwangju uprising and the other events of the 1980 military coup. Wickham, in good military style, spoke in matter-of-fact terms and showed little inclination to second-guess earlier decisions. Gleysteen, a scholarly diplomat, was highly retrospective and willing to entertain questions about any number of alternatives that they could have or should have considered. They both made a point of stating that they worked together closely and in harmony in making the decisions they made.

Their position is that the coup of December 12, 1979, in which Chun Doo Hwan took complete control of the Korean military, was so well executed that they had little choice but to accept it. Although the handling of the Kwangju uprising in May, 1980 was a striking failure on the part of the new military hierarchy and the wounds of Kwangju still plague the government, the crushing of the Kwangju uprising was one step in what amounted to a coup d'etat by stages. It was one of a series of events that began in December and culminated in Chun's election as president the next August.

The criticism of American actions also extends back in time to the response to the December 12 events. The most reasonable way to have prevented the Kwangju Uprising would have been to prevent or counter the coup on December 12. Why did the U.S. officials not do more to prevent the coup from taking place?

The descriptions provided by Gleysteen and Wickham of the events of that night make it clear that the Korean army, under its senior leadership, could not have stopped the well-planned, well-executed coup by Chun and his cohorts. How then could the United States? Gleysteen was called to the U.S. Eighth Army's command bunker on South Post in Yongsan around 7:30 p.m.; Wickham had arrived there just minutes before. From sources which included American units in the area of the DMZ and southward where the R.O.K. Army had been stationed or had moved through, they knew that troops were moving on Seoul. Beyond that they knew only that the troops were not North Korean. Around 9:00 p.m. the Minister of Defense, No Che-hyon, entered the bunker along with Kim Chong-hwan, the Chairman of the R.O.K. Joint Chiefs of Staff Before long they were able to establish that the troops on the move were under the control of Major General Chun Doo Hwan, the Army Security Commander, then acting as director of the Martial Law Command's investigation of President Park's assassination. One option was for the senior Korean officials to call out other units to confront Chun's troops in the streets of Seoul. They first began to exercise that option but General Wickham urged that they wait until dawn. (They also may have recognized that Chun could thwart such orders through his own chain of command, the Defense Security officers assigned to the field units.)

Later that evening Defense Minister No and JCS Chairman Kim were asked by the coup leaders to come out of the bunker and report to the Ministry of Defense building. Wickham and Gleysteen urged them not to go, but they left. The two were arrested after an assault on the Ministry of Defense and forced to go along with President Ch'oe Kyu-ha in signing arrest warrants for General Chong Sung-hwa and others. (It is important to note that General Chong Sung-hwa, who was acting as the martial law commander under the Constitution, was arrested with violence by the coup leaders before the president authorized the arrest.)

Chong Sung-hwa subsequently was accused of complicity in the assassination of President Park Chung Hee. He was present (although in an adjoining building) on the night Park was shot, and had subsequently become the martial law commander. Chong was arrested and jailed on December 12.

One version of why he was arrested is that he was about to order Chun Doo Hwan to be transferred to a remote command on the East Coat, in effect banishing him, and that the coup against him was set in motion when word of the impending transfer reached Chun. In any event, the charges against him were very serious. (His life may have been saved, inadvertently, by Wickham, who sent him a birthday card, as Wickham did routinely for his counterparts, even though Chong was in jail. Chun Doo Hwan immediately went to Gleysteen to heatedly demand an explanation for Wickham's interference in Korean domestic affairs. Chong, for his part, wept when he received the card because he interpreted it as Wickham's assurance that he, Chong, would not be executed.) Ultimately he was sentenced to twenty years in prison but then set free for health reasons.

Coup rumors had been fed to Wickham, and he passed them on to the ROK Army and Ministry of Defense. Their response was disbelief and disregard, as if to ask, "How could an American possibly know something like that before the Koreans themselves."

After the coup, Chun called on Gleysteen first, and then, a day or two later, on Wickham. His message was that they were "going to clean up the corruption, after which they would return to the barracks." Chun said, "Trust me; watch what we do, and you will be proud of me someday." Gleysteen and Wickham were both suspicious of the general's message. Wickham checked the files and found that when Park staged his coup in 1961, he had sent Kim Chong-p'il to see General Carter B. Magruder, then the United Nations Commander in Seoul. Magruder's report to the Commander-in-Chief for the Pacific in Hawaii was that Kim had told him that they were "going to clean up the corruption, after which they would return to the barracks." Kim had said, "Trust us; watch what we do, and you will be proud of us someday."

And yet Chun and his colleagues swore that they had no political ambitions. They claimed that the coup was strictly a military matter; a house-cleaning to get rid of corrupt civilian leaders and older generals, some of whom had been at the four-star level for as long as twenty-four years. The younger generals, Chun and others, claimed that they were just clearing the way for room at the top.

Why didn't Americans act on their suspicions of an impending coup? Apparently they did, at least within the limits of the options they perceived available to them. Although publicly they seemed to cooperate with the new group of generals, privately they criticized them. The generals rejected the criticism, claiming interference in domestic affairs. Some of the American dissatisfaction spilled into the press but without official condemnation from Washington.

Gleysteen had set his contingency plans should a coup occur while he was in Korea. His concerns were, first, to prevent fighting, second, to prevent North Korean intervention, and third, to minimize the political destruction. His goals in addressing these concerns included a three-point plan: (1) to reduce the costs (bloodshed), (2) to get in touch with the leaders of the coup (without which influence would be impossible), and (3) keep the United States from being put in a foolish position. On the last point, Gleysteen was concerned that the United States not look bad, as it had at the time of the 1961 coup. In 1961, General Magruder, exercising his operational authority as United Nations Commander, had actually ordered General Park Chung Hee to return to the barracks, which in retrospect was a useless and naive move. Since the organizers of the coup were willing to face guns and death, they were not about to bow to a foreigner's orders.

In examining the American position, several questions arise. Should the U.S. have known? A coup by its very nature, by definition, is a sudden and secret action by armed soldiers willing to kill or be killed. Rumors were heard by the Americans but were discounted by their high-ranking Korean counterparts.

Could the U.S. have done more on the night of December 12, 1979? Gleysteen has related that messages from Washington urged issuing of orders for the soldiers to return to their assigned areas. Such orders would have been would have been ignored, just as they were during Park's coup in May, 1961.

In the following days, what should the U.S. have done? Gleysteen steered the U.S. through a series of decisions which first called for a waiting period to determine where the balance of power lay. Then, upon identifying the power behind the coup, he decided how to deal with them. He felt that keeping the lines of communication open was the key to any hope of influencing the outcome. He thought that a dual approach, with one line to Chun and one to President Ch'oe Kyu-ha, would be most productive. Gleysteen called on Ch'oe on the morning of December 13, and he says that even then it was clear that Ch'oe was not "an independent actor."

On the afternoon of December 13, General Chun came to visit Gleysteen at the Ambassador's residence in Chong-dong. He said that it was a fight between soldiers, young vs. old.

He promised that they would not interfere with the democratic process and would not foul the constitutional
institutions nor processes. Chun went on to say he would not
become the president and he was indeed critical of Park
Chung Hee, saying that Park had tried to hold onto power too
long.

Over the next few days, having identified and evaluated
the power base of the new coup, the United States had
roughly three options: (1) active involvement, including
supporting a counter-coup, (2) do nothing, and (3) issue
warnings and watch unhappily. The options were limited
because of the strength and uniform support throughout the
Korean military for the coup. Gleysteen says the U.S. was
amazed at the solidity of support within the military for
Chun's group. They could not find a significant alternative
group for a counter-coup. Wickham at one point stated that
they were approached by some who asked for support for a
counter-coup, but they "sent them packing," implying that
they did not see, to have the support necessary within the
military to succeed.

Doing nothing was not an appealing option. The American
Embassy in consultation with Washington chose to try to
limit the damage of the new coup by trying to work with the
coup leaders quietly at most times, but occasionally openly.
For example, in April 1980, when Chun violated the Korean
constitution and appointed himself acting head of the KCIA,
the U.S. openly and strongly criticized the action.

The next step in the mounting of the coup was the
arrest of the three Kims and the expansion of martial law on
the night of May 17 and the morning of May 18, 1980--the
events that led to the Kwangju Uprising. The U.S. demanded
the release of the Kims; and the demand was given to Martial
Law Commander Yi Hui-song as well as to President Ch'oe
Kyu-ha. The demands were made public in Washington as well
as through the USIS system (four offices in Seoul, Pusan,
Taegu and Kwangju). The action went unnoticed in the
violence and the uprising to follow in Kwangju. Gleysteen
has recently written that the Embassy did not heed the
developments in Kwangju initially because, "Ironically, we
were distracted at the time in Seoul with a very strong
protest against Kim [Dae Jung]'s arrest."

He goes on to write, "Both the Embassy and the U.S.
military command learned of the affair after the crucial
damage was already done. Without our knowledge, the Korean
authorities decided to cope with the tumultuous, but not
particularly violent, demonstrations in Kwangju by
reinforcing police with army special warfare units, which

were not and have never been under U.S. [UN/CFC] command. The Black Berets used highly provocative tactics which infuriated the people of Kwangju, causing a rapid escalation of violence and killing, forcing the government forces to withdraw for several days to a security perimeter around the city."

In describing American actions once the Korean army had been driven from the city, Gleysteen writes, "Frustrated by our limited influence and ignorant of what was going on, the U.S. government in Seoul and Washington immediately deplored the violence and encouraged a peaceful settlement. We strongly endorsed efforts by the Catholic archbishop to mediate a settlement, which until the last two days held some hope of success. We leaned as hard as we could on the Korean army to keep talking and minimize any further violence."

As Gleysteen's article continues, he writes of an episode that in retrospect was of critical importance in the ultimate perception of the U.S. role in Kwangju. He writes, " . . . we issued a number of public statements, including a carefully crafted one calling on both sides to settle the issue peacefully and warning North Korea not to meddle. The Korean authorities agreed to broadcast and airdrop the statement, which was well publicized in the U.S. media. However, few if any Kwangju residents heard or read our statement, while many of them heard disinformation that the U.S. facilitated and supported the repression. I can only speculate as to who was responsible for this nasty twist."

Of course, it was not in the interests of the martial law forces to drop the promised leaflets stating the U.S. urged mediation. The military wanted it to appear that the U.S. was supporting their efforts.

The next event, the release from the US-ROK Combined Forces Command of the R.O.K. Twentieth Infantry Division from its duties in the Seoul area, further fed suspicions that the U.S. was in league with the Korean military. Wickham explained the action as a response to a request from the Minister of Defense and as a means of cooperating with the military in controlling a situation that needed to be "nipped in the bud." Gleysteen explained their giving permission for the Twentieth Division to be released from Combined Forces Command was contingent on its being used only if negotiations in Kwangju broke down. Gleysteen also felt that since the Twentieth had had riot control training, unlike the Black Berets, they would be able to retake the city without inciting greater violence. The U.S. did urge the military to wait and allow the negotiations a chance to

work. Although we do not know how long they delayed, the
Embassy had the impression that they had obtained about two
days of delay. Eventually the Twentieth retook the city
with little resistance except for a few holdouts at the
toch'ong; about thirty died.

Gleysteen reported, "Almost immediately, and acting
without instructions, I urged the government at a high level
to apologize or at least express deep regret for what
happened at Kwangju. It did not do so, presumably for fear
that the slightest acknowledgement of error would unravel
its web of authority."

Gleysteen concludes his reflections on the Kwangju
uprising by saying, "Not much was said praising or criticiz-
ing the U.S. at the time. Within a few months, however, a
myth sprang up in Kwangju that the U.S. was partly
responsible for the incident. The timing postdated the
Reagan-Chun summit meeting, suggesting that act may have
provoked someone to maliciously disseminate false charges
against the U.S."

Wickham and Gleysteen, in my interviews with them,
indicated concern for the "myths" that had grown, or in
other words they were concerned with the way history was
being recorded. Both the opposition and military have used
the U.S. for their own purposes. For the opposition,
criticism of the U.S. has become a corollary for any
criticism of the current government. For the government,
appreciation expressed for the Reagan summit and other
actions have given the impression that the government wants
the Korean people to believe it has U.S. support.

The events of the Kwangju uprising have herein been
described as part of a chain of events that began with the
December 12 intra-military coup. Kwangju was located at a
midpoint with the events of August 1980 as a kind of
culmination. Chun came to the fore after having toyed with
the idea of remaining behind the scenes, as a "Shogun,"
while allowing civilian government to remain as a facade.
The process whereby Chun became a civilian president is also
associated with General Wickham. On August 8, 1980, the Los
Angeles Times and Associated Press ran stories quoting an
anonymous high-ranking military officer as saying that the
U.S. would indeed support another military-style government
in Korea. The article included the famous "lemming" remark,
the statement that Koreans always line up behind their
leaders and were doing so for Chun.

General Wickham, in meeting with me, was interested in
relating this incident for the record. As events unfolded in
1980, Ambassador Gleysteen urged Wickham to meet with news-

men periodically in order to pass along information on developments because it was difficult for the media to keep current. In August, General Wickham met with two reporters, Terry Anderson of the Associated Press (who is currently being held hostage in Lebanon) and Sam Jameson of the <u>Los Angeles Times</u>. That interview clearly was understood as taking place "off the record" and "for background only;" however, as is his practice with interviews, Wickham did allow the conversation to be recorded. As a final question, after Anderson and Jameson had stood to leave, Anderson asked if the United States would support another military leader in Korea. Wickham responded with what was being discussed in State Department circles: that the new military leaders in Korea would have to go through a legitimizing process involving an election, and would have to demonstrate that they had the support of the majority of the people. If such conditions were met, said Wickham, the U.S. probably would support the new government. The reporters took these remarks of the general as a scoop and ran stories with the headlines "U.S. Support Claimed for S.[outh] Korea's Chun."

The next day, Henry Scott Stokes of the <u>New York Times</u>, who was rooming in the same place as Anderson and Jameson, took the tape with him to an interview with General Chun Doo Hwan. He played the tape for Chun, and asked him who was speaking. Then, feeling clear of the obligation of confidentiality promised by Anderson and Jameson, Stokes reported that Chun had identified Wickham as the source of the quotations. Within two weeks, Chun forced Ch'oe Kyu-ha to resign and took the office of interim president for himself. A short while later he was "elected" in his own right by the electoral college.

And once again through either manipulation by Korean government officials or through mistakes by the Americans or a combination of the above, the United States was again portrayed as supportive of the military coup and the Chun government in Korea. Both Wickham and Gleysteen have stated clearly that supporting the coup was not their intention; but later they came to work with the coup because they saw no reasonable alternative. They had tried everything short of drastic action and they feared that drastic action would yield drastic or uncertain or even unacceptable results. It was revealing to me that they both talked of possible counter-coups, and they both spoke of the surprising effectiveness of the Chun coup. It was well-planned, well-executed and well-supported. Only drastic alternatives remained, and they were too risky, given the realities of the situation and the dangerous North Korean threat.

In retrospect and given the growth of anti-Americanism in Korea, perhaps the United States would have been better off looking "foolish," but Gleysteen chose to avoid this in order to have influence on the military after the coup. In his view, American influence was marginal--both in the sense of effectiveness and in the sense of being on the periphery. Whereas Wickham was less concerned with anti-Americanism (he considers it a natural outgrowth of relationships between two countries, one of which is catching up to the other economically), Gleysteen was concerned about the blame leveled at the U.S. from both sides of the spectrum in Korea. Irrespective of the facts, there is political advantage to both sides in keeping the U.S. in the center of the controversy.

The complete history of Kwangju will not be known until Koreans at all levels of involvement are able to speak freely about it or until hidden documents can be brought to light and studied. At this point, with the press accounts and eyewitness accounts at the time available to us, and now with the American officials beginning to reveal what they know, we are closer to being able to write an accurate history of the event. More will be revealed when government classified documents become available and when participants feel free to talk about it openly. For now, seven years after the event, the dispassionate historian is still limited in writing an objective history of the Kwangju uprising.

NOTES

[1]When tried under martial law, Kim was found guilty and sentenced to death. The sentence was eventually commuted to "life," and then to twenty years. U.S. official opinion that the charges were "far-fetched" encouraged the reduction. In fact Kim was allowed to spend two years in exile in the U.S., followed by two years of house arrest and then restoration of his civil rights as part of the "democratization" of Korea in the summer of 1987.

[2]William H. Gleysteen, Jr., "Korea: A Special Target of American Concern," in David D. Newsom (ed.) The Diplomacy of Human Rights (Lanham, Md.: University Press of America, 1986), pp. 85-99.

Commentary:
Interpreting the Kwangju Uprising

Donald N. Clark

To speak of Kwangju is to open a wound in modern Korean life. Experience suggests that we will never know the full story of what happened there in May, 1980. It is unlikely that we will ever know exactly how many people died in the fighting; nor will we ever know the full extent to which American influence was a factor in the uprising and the repression which crushed it. Yet clearly Kwangju remains a potent symbol of the failed promise of democracy in Korea, and as such carries great emotional, as well as political, significance. To ignore what happened in Kwangju while attempting to understand the continuing flow of history in modern Korea is to risk continued misunderstanding and perhaps even a repetition of the event during some future political upheaval.

In this volume, Koreanists Linda Lewis, David McCann, and Mark Peterson have gone a long way toward defining the issues and enhancing our understanding of what happened, and why. All three are sensitive and sympathetic observers of Korea with considerable analytical experience. In approaching Kwangju from the point of view of their respective disciplines, they ask whether their traditional methodologies have much use in instances where sheer rage and violence obliterate the neat categories of academic discourse. How can the event be sorted out and its effect on the contemporary Korean scene be taken into account?

WHAT HAPPENED AND WHY

Linda Lewis and David McCann both cite the work of Elizabeth Perry on peasant movements in north China. Much of what Perry says, like much of China scholarship in general,

65

Conclusion

1984

is helpful in explaining patterns in Korea as well. However, Kwangju was an urban revolt, an uprising by educated people, by students destined for elite status and success. Among many differences one might cite the impact of news coverage on the event: the fact that when the government-controlled television networks misrepresented what was happening and thus interfered with a key aim of the Kwangju demonstrators --the gathering of nationwide public support against the military regime--the people suddenly realized that government control was more than just guns and tanks, but thought control as well, through television. This was a thoroughly "modern" lesson, and though accounts like Perry's of peasant rebellion may help us a little, what we really need is a better-organized inquiry into what has happened to people like the Koreans, who have moved so rapidly through so many stages of modernization. To what extent <u>had</u> the people of Kwangju, while living far from the metropolis of Seoul and retaining at least some of their rural outlook, been lulled by methods of mass communications into acceptance of the developing new government? What was it like to realize in the spring of 1980 that the new government was going to perpetuate the prejudice against them, to view them as peripheral people who could never be trusted--and whose political candidate, Kim Dae Jung, could not be trusted--with the responsibilities of full participation?

Lewis and McCann look to their direct experience to find explanations for why peaceful protest so rapidly escalated into deadly street fighting. Both of them refer to the classic pattern of the public altercation in village Korea, in which the antagonists appear to be coming to blows, but at the last minute are prevented from doing so by friends who step in to separate them. Ultimately the dispute is settled through negotiations and the intercession of friends and relatives. The pattern is a type of survival mechanism for the community, since the antagonists must continue living together in the community. Village life would be intolerable if virtually any argument could develop into a violent fight. There would be no time for anything but the settling of scores.

These observations are valid. Where Lewis and McCann give us more to think about is in their extrapolation of this pattern to the Kwangju case, to suggest that the people of Kwangju somehow expected the Americans to intervene to save them from the oncoming confrontation with the R.O.K. Army. In the village fight model, people say terrible things --real "fighting words"--to each other, knowing that the

ensuing fight will not be allowed to happen. In Kwangju, if
this notion is at all valid, the people made a terrible
mistake in thinking that the United States--even under the
Carter administration with its avowed concern for human
rights--would (or could) intervene so openly in Korean
affairs. When Linda Lewis writes of her surprise at the
suggestion that people expected the U.S. to do this, I
expect she means that she thought it was a dangerous thing
for her friends in Kwangju to expect.

Another example of this sort of cultural extrapolation
is Lewis's notion that the people of Kwangju, thinking
themselves innocent and abused, took on an attitude
equivalent to that of a battered wife who excuses her
violent husband because he has been drinking. If she can
blame the alcohol, then she can avoid the more painful
questions about her life and marriage. This kind of reaction
is not, of course, uniquely Korean.

In superimposing this pattern on the middle class of
Kwangju, which came out in support of the students after the
Black Berets beat and stabbed unarmed people in the streets,
Lewis helps us understand that rebellion against the
government was very difficult for many citizens. Beyond the
terror of facing armed and angry soldiers with nothing more
than moral force, the office workers and church members of
Kwangju needed to believe that their "marriage" was still
fundamentally stable; that the ideals of their modern,
independent republic made a difference in how Koreans could
expect to be treated by their government.

In recounting her conversations with people in Kwangju,
Lewis gives us a picture of citizens watching events in
proverbial shock and disbelief. Sixty-one years after the
March First Independence Movement and half a century after
their grandparents and parents rose up against the Japanese
colonial authorities for abusing them in their own town, how
could it happen that South Korean soldiers could come into
Kwangju shooting to kill citizens who once again were
demonstrating for their freedom? Perhaps they were not
really "our" soldiers. Perhaps, like the Japanese in 1919
and 1929 and the North Korean Communists in 1950, they were
an enemy force, perhaps drawn from the rival Yongnam region.
Thus the rumor flew around that the Black Berets had been
chosen because they were natives of the Kyongsang provinces,
fed liquor and drugs, and sent into the city to terrorize
the people into submission. How absurd for any regime
capable of such a crime to expect public support when it
declared itself a "democracy" following a one-candidate
election! This is the flavor of much of the literature about

Kwangju which has been circulating underground and on campuses throughout the 1980's in South Korea.

THE KOREAN GOVERNMENT POSITION

Given these facts, the rage in Kwangju is easy to understand. However, the Chun government publicly puts forth a provocative explanation for what happened. Its position, expressed in various backgrounders (see bibliography), is that the events of Kwangju were the work of a planning group which kept close touch with the political opposition in Seoul, namely Kim Dae Jung, and drew financing from various suspicious sources. In this volume we offer also the government's official account of the events in Kwangju in May 1980. The government presents an "outside agitator" theory. "Impure elements" set the situation up. Rock-throwing students stormed government arsenals and seized weapons with which to extort popular support at gunpoint, according to the government account. Despite great restraint on the part of the Korean army, many people--civilians, police, and soldiers--lost their lives as the government sorrowfully but justifiably used force to restore order. The government points to many attempts which were made to reason with the rioters, to visits to the city by Prime Minister Shin Hyon-hwak and President Ch'oe Kyu-ha. The moderate citizens' committee tried its best to negotiate a peaceful end to the incident, but radical elements frustrated their efforts and chose to push the affair to its violent conclusion. Having no choice, then, the government took the city with military force and, having done so, assisted grieving families with indemnities and funeral funds. The unhappy incident is now history. To reopen the discussion is to inflict needless agony on the victims' families. To heal the wounds, the incident should be put to rest.

This view is shared by certain American conservatives who have influence with the Reagan administration in matters of East Asian policy. Daryl M. Plunk, a policy analyst with the Heritage Foundation, put it this way in a 1985 background paper on Kwangju:

> The events of May 1980 were not a deliberate plot by the ROK government to massacre innocent civilians in South Cholla Province. Nor was the U.S. involved in the incident. Given the extent of the insurrection, the death toll was remarkably low--a fact that reflects the ROK government's efforts to

[handwritten margin note: Valid reasons to impose Martial Law again? Student demonstrations?]

minimize casualties. Those who continue to distort
what happened at Kwangju should have their motives
questioned. They seem determined to prevent the
wounds from healing and to drive a wedge between
the U.S. and the Korean people. The ROK government,
by contrast, has been trying to put the Kwangju
incident to rest and to heal the country's physical
and emotional wounds. (Emphasis added)[1]

The essential silliness of the "Lay it to rest" school
was demonstrated by events in Korea in the summer of 1987,
which revealed what Koreans have really felt since 1979
about the Chun regime and its method of taking power.
Clearly it cannot be laid to rest. Indeed, there is no
understanding contemporary Korean affairs without taking it
up. What is more, by not taking it up, we risk the
continuation of some serious misunderstandings in American-
Korean relations.

THE AMERICAN CONNECTION

A dismaying by-product of the Kwangju incident is the
fact that so many Koreans believe that the United States
government had some connection with what happened, and
countenanced it. So many people believe that there was--or
should have been, as Linda Lewis has described the views of
some of her friends--an American role somewhere in the
incident, that it is important for the U.S. government to
confront the matter realistically and consistently, without
resort to exotic technicalities about the structure of the
US-ROK Combined Forces Command.
Mark Peterson has given us a most significant treatment
of this issue based on personal contact with Ambassador
William H. Gleysteen and General John A. Wickham, the senior
American officials on the scene who have become the villains
in the Korean students' version of Kwangju. It is not the
first time that Gleysteen, at least, has gone on record with
his version of events--that things happened too fast for the
U.S. to be able to deflect the actions of the Chun group in
the R.O.K. military.
Here it is important to point to Peterson's treatment
of Chun's December 12, 1979 coup d'etat. We argue in this
book that the Kwangju incident was part of a longer process:
as Chun took control of the military by violence on the
night of December 12th, he took control of the Korean
populace in Kwangju between May 18 and May 27. The decisions

that were made with respect to Kwangju in May were made by people who seized power in December. Gleysteen may well be correct in asserting that the R.O.K. military had every right, even within the structure of the Combined Forces Command, to assign the Twentieth Division to the recapture of Kwangju in May, since the redeployment of those troops did not endanger security on the peninsula. The more difficult problem arises from what the Americans said and did when Chun used troops from the forward defense areas to seize the Defense Ministry and the R.O.K. Army Headquarters at Yongsan on the night of December 12th. As Peterson tells it, Ambassador Gleysteen and General Wickham had no prior knowledge of events that night, apparently had little guidance from Washington, and spent the evening in the bunker on South Post feeling relieved that the North Koreans were not involved. Beyond that, they were completely without power to influence events.

THE PROBLEM OF THE COMBINED FORCES COMMAND

Korean dissidents and persons joining the anti-American current which has been flowing in South Korea might find it pallid to encounter legal technicalities in a discussion of something as obvious as the scale of American influence in Korea; yet it is important to address the legal position of the American officials in Korea before assigning blame to them personally for not using their authority to stop Chun from taking over the military and then the entire government in 1979-80. They (and the U.S. government) are accused of wanting to maintain stability and military security no matter what the cost to the Korean people, and hence of countenancing Chun's coup and the subsequent massacre in Kwangju as one price to be paid for the protection of American interests in Korea. The key question, therefore, is whether they voluntarily stood aside when they should have tried to intervene to put the American military and moral presence in Korea in Chun's way. This requires a brief analysis of the command relationships in Korea.

Since the truce which ended the Korean War, peace in Korea has been assured by the United Nations Command. The U.N.C. was created in 1950 by the United Nations Security Council, which specified that the U.N. Commander should be someone appointed by the President of the United States-- a senior American officer. At the same time, for reasons of military necessity, President Syngman Rhee put Korean forces under the operational control of the U.N.C. as well.

Strategic defense of the peninsula has been based since that
time on the concept of a unified command in wartime, under
the U.N.C. structure headed by an American.

Since the mid-1950's, however, the United Nations have
been reducing their presence in Korea while R.O.K. forces
have been growing in numbers and capability. Although the
United States maintains significant Army and Air Force units
in Korea--troop strength is understood to be around 40,000
--they are small compared to the roughly 620,000 South
Koreans on active duty and the nearly 4.8 million men in the
service reserves and Homeland Reserve Force. Although the
U.N. Commander--always an American--may be said to command
in wartime and to have exclusive control over such things as
nuclear weapons in peacetime, it is hardly plausible that he
could oppose the wishes of the Korean military for long.

In 1978, the United States and Korea created the US-ROK
Combined Forces Command (C.F.C.). This eclipsed the U.N.C.,
which nevertheless continues in existence to act as the
agent of the southern side at the armistice talks at
P'anmunjom. The C.F.C., while retaining an American
Commander-in-Chief, allows for increased sharing of
command authority between officers from both sides. Table 1
on page 72, adapted from a monograph on the C.F.C. by
Brigadier General Taek-hyung Rhee of the R.O.K. Army, shows
how key positions in the C.F.C. are apportioned.

The table shows several interesting things. Every
office has a chief and a deputy. The command echelons have
American chiefs and Korean deputies, while lower echelons
sometimes have Korean chiefs. Americans thus appear to
command the staff, planning, and operations functions of the
C.F.C. This keeps Americans involved in strategic defense
and is consistent with the history of the joint command.
However the chart also suggests that Americans are in a
weaker position when it comes to personnel (i.e., not much
help in keeping R.O.K. officers from moving around in
preparation for a coup) and intelligence (i.e., not
necessarily the first to get information about military
affairs in the peninsula).

Table 2 on page 73 combines information from two
diagrams in General Rhee's study describing the flow of
authority through the Combined Forces Command in peacetime.
It shows that the C.F.C., under the joint US-ROK Military
Committee, had "operational control" over R.O.K. combat
troops in Korea in 1979-80. Indeed, the Americans in the
C.F.C. would seem theoretically to have been in a position
to block the December 12 coup--or at least to order General
Roh Tae Woo's Ninth Division back to duty on the front line.

However, the problem lies in the lines of "command without control," which descend parallel to the C.F.C. from the R.O.K. Ministry of Defense to R.O.K. forces, giving the Korean Defense Minister and Chiefs of Staff "command without operational control" over R.O.K. forces. Obviously the Koreans have voluntarily relinquished this operational authority, and they can just as voluntarily take it back again whenever they choose, since the lines of "command without operational control" are all in place.

TABLE 1
Organization and Operation of C.F.C. Headquarters

Division	Position	Chief	Deputy
Operational Command Positions	Commander-in-Chief	U.S.	R.O.K.
	Chief of Staff	U.S.	R.O.K.
	Planning	U.S.	R.O.K.
	Operations	U.S.	R.O.K.
Combat Support Positions	Personnel	R.O.K.	U.S.
	Intelligence	R.O.K.	U.S.
	Logistics	U.S.	R.O.K.
	Communications	R.O.K.	U.S.
	Engineers	R.O.K.	U.S.
	Operational Analysis Group	R.O.K.	U.S.
	Judge Advocate	U.S.	R.O.K.
	Public Affairs	U.S.	R.O.K.
	Headquarters Commandant	R.O.K.	U.S.
	Secretary, Combined Staff	U.S.	R.O.K.
Subtotals		R.O.K.-7 U.S. - 7	U.S. - 7 R.O.K.-7

Total officers assigned to C.F.C. Headquarters:
182 Korean; 133 U.S.

Source: Taek-hyung Rhee, US-ROK Combined Operations: a Korean Perspective (Washington, D.C.: National Defense University, 1986), p. 45.

TABLE 2
Command Relationships Within the Combined Forces Command

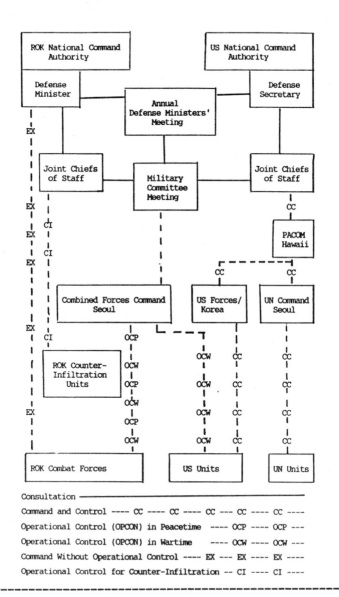

Source: Rhee, pp. 34–38.

Ultimately it matters little whose side held the authority to block the December coup, since the key officers on the R.O.K. side were in the bunker with the Americans while the coup was taking place out in the streets. As Peterson and others describe it, Defense Minister No Che-hyon had no choice but to emerge and order the arrest of Army Chief of Staff Chong Sung-hwa, thereby turning the army over to the coup leaders.

The Combined Forces Command seems like a model organization, but it raises certain contradictions. The command structure puts American officers in charge of operations. But all other signs point to a situation in which Americans bear responsibility but do not have real control. On one hand, one can hardly argue that Americans lack influence in Korean affairs. On a broad spectrum of issues the Koreans look to the United States for guidance and are susceptible to American suggestion. However, in the military sphere, the American command seems to have been nudged upstairs, where it is subject to manipulation against its better judgment.

There are two ways to look at the relationships in the Combined Forces Command. One is to assume that the structure will be scrupulously honored by both sides and that it is an effective way to coordinate defense. The other is to see it as a snare for the American side, designed to assure U.S. support for whatever the Korean military wishes to accomplish. From the GI standing guard near Munsan-ni to the topmost brass in the offices overlooking the Yongsan parade field, the structure is designed to draw the American people and their Congress into whatever goes wrong with the Korean armistice. But a potentially dangerous feature of the joint defense structure is that it can be used to get U.S. support for whatever the R.O.K. military wants to accomplish, even it if is unrelated to national defense. As the Korean military has found political roles to play, the Americans have had to follow along or else oppose them openly. So far that has not been desirable.

Thus the American commander relies for information about what is happening in Korea upon intelligence from within the R.O.K. military, which can keep him in the dark if it chooses. The Combined Forces Command obviously is no better than the Korean officers want it to be, and the Americans are reduced to trusting them not to use the command structure for domestic political purposes.

But this is still not enough to explain the position of the U.S. military on the Korean scene. Although it seems to be American policy to claim that our officials in Seoul have little influence in Korean affairs, and the workings of the C.F.C. tend to bear this out, a better way to say it would be that while Americans may have little influence on the routine of Korean politics, in moments of crisis their influence is critical. This is true despite the human tendency of American officials to act in confused and contradictory ways during a crisis. Consider Mark Peterson's description of the scene in the American command bunker on South Post on the night of December 12: how Wickham and Gleysteen did not know the origin or identity of the units moving on Seoul; how they tried to protect the senior Korean military officials; how they tried to dissuade them from going out into the fray; how Wickham later may unwittingly have saved the life of Chong Sung-hwa by sending him a birthday card; and later still how Wickham seemed to bless the Chun forces by referring to the Korean military as the stewards of Korean constitutionality. Did the American officials really mean to nurture a new military dictatorship in Korea? Surely not. But is it any wonder that the military under Chun felt no restraint from the United States when they decided to crush the May uprising in Kwangju with overwhelming military force? And is it any wonder that so many Koreans now believe that American policy had something to do with the death of their hopes for reform in 1980?

General Wickham's actions throughout the period are difficult to excuse, particularly in light of the American claim of non-interference in Korean domestic affairs. Clearly his words and deeds encouraged the Chun forces to believe that the Combined Forces Command--and presumably the entire American policy apparatus--would acquiesce in his taking over the country rather than block his way and put stability in the peninsula at risk. In Peterson's account it is especially shocking to learn how American journalists may have played a key role in conveying to Chun the American commander's private thoughts, even though Wickham again might be blamed for being so candid. But if the American general was a participant in the events that brought Chun to power, it is at least partly because the Combined Forces Command is set up so that the American Commander-in-Chief can only help the Korean military do what it wants to do.

CONCLUSION

The direction to take in critiquing the American role in Kwangju, therefore, is to critique the arrangements in the Combined Forces Command. If the Americans can be drawn

into even tacit support for any general who can muster
enough guns to storm the Defense Ministry on a winter night
in downtown Seoul and who then fails to restrain his faction
from turning those guns on the South Korean people, surely
it is time to reassess the American military presence in
Korea and to ask whether it is still in our interest to
maintain a force which has become so vulnerable to domestic
political manipulation. At the very least we should take
steps to protect our American public servants from
arrangements with foreign governments which may make them
culpable for atrocities committed by local troops whom they
command but cannot possibly control.

NOTES

[1] The Heritage Foundation, "South Korea's Kwangju
Incident--Revisited," Asian Studies Center Backgrounder No.
35 (September 16, 1985), p. 7.

[2] Taek-hyung Rhee, US-ROK Combined Operations: a Korean
Perspective (Washington, D.C.: National Defense University,
1986). General Rhee's monograph contains much of interest on
this subject, including (for example) the criticism of the
Americans for putting an Air Force General (representing the
next-most-important U.S. service branch in Korea) in the
position of C.F.C. Chief of Staff, who is to take charge of
the Ground Component Command (i.e., the R.O.K. Army) in case
of war. Such arrangements suggest that the staff structure
may be determined as much by service rivalries as by
concerns about the strategic defense of Korea. The more
important point is that the Koreans themselves question the
value of these arrangements.

Commentary:
Kwangju and the Korean People

Chong-Sik Lee

At first I hesitated to accept the invitation to participate in this panel because I was not sure that we could deal with the Kwangju Incident as an academic subject. I was afraid that we might be too close to the scene. The memory of what happened is too vividly burnt into our memory. Who could forget the tragic scenes of May 1980 telecast in vivid color day after day? Who could forget the brutal scenes depicted in color spreads in the news magazines? How could we discuss such things with scholarly objectivity?

But the papers presented in the panel make significant contributions to our understanding of the tragic event, and I wish to congratulate all those involved in organizing the panel. These are my thoughts upon reading the papers.

WHAT HAPPENED IN KWANGJU

Linda Lewis and Mark Peterson contribute much to our our understanding of the facts concerning the events at Kwangju. The controversy surrounding the number of people killed there in May 1980 has created the impression that there are differences of opinion concerning the facts of the Kwangju incident; but in fact their accounts and that of the Martial Law Command are in substantial agreement that (1) the tragedy began with student demonstrations; (2) that the demonstrations were brutally suppressed by contingents of the Special Forces, or Black Berets; (3) that this led to the citizens' rallies and the siege and (4) the final assault by the army. This agreement makes it easier for us to sort out the events.

WHAT WAS KWANGJU?

There seems to be no agreement, however, on how to characterize the events of May 1980. How should we refer to them? Linda Lewis called it a "rebellion," but David McCann said that the word "rebellion" is too chaste a term for what happened. "Uprising is even less satisfactory," according to McCann. He equates the Kwangju incident with the sexual torture of a woman prisoner in 1986 and the torture death of a student prisoner in 1987. It is going to be difficult to find agreement now or in the future on this point. The term one uses to characterize the events in Kwangju will tell more about the person who is using it than about the events themselves. There is no doubt, however, that it was a tragedy of great magnitude in Korean history.

WHY KWANGJU? WHY DID IT HAPPEN?

We can analyze the events on three levels:

1. Why did the students demonstrate?
2. Why did the paratroopers behave so savagely?
3. Why did the citizens join the students?

The first and last questions are probably much easier to answer than the second one. Given President Park's assassination in October 1979 and the events that followed, student demonstrations were something to be expected—with or without Kim Dae Jung's instigation. I mention the last point because the Martial Law Command accused him of malicious instigation and sentenced him to death for it. And then, given the savagery of the paratroopers that most of us witnessed on TV, the participation of the ordinary citizenry can be readily understood. Linda Lewis observes that even civil servants joined the ranks of indignant citizens. We are told that the people were "outraged," not only by the initial savagery but also by the government's refusal to apologize or in any way to acknowledge that it was an excessive use of force. Lewis and McCann agree that persistent distortions in the Korean news reports of the events also inflamed the citizens of Kwangju.

But why did the Black Berets treat the students in Kwangju as if they were sworn enemies of the Republic? Lewis suggests the possibility that they were drunk and did not know what they were doing. We have heard other rumors concerning the Black Berets' behavior also. The Martial Law

Command, on the other hand, blamed the "excesses" on the
heated atmosphere. I cannot say that I am convinced by these
theories and explanations. However, one thing is certain.
Future attempts to explain the Special Forces' behavior will
be enormously painful. Many years will pass before we can
approach the question with dispassion. It will take statesmanship of the highest caliber to heal the wounds inflicted
by those rash young men on that fateful day. Peterson says
that the "Kwangju uprising will not be resolved until the
dead can be properly honored." And yet we do not even know
how many actually died during those tragic days.

David McCann goes beyond the ground level and links the
events in Kwangju in the historical and geographic context
of Kwangju and the Cholla provinces. He says it was a case
of the center looking for "disorder" (ran) on the periphery
and the periphery feeling "resentment" (han). This is a
potent theme. The rivalry between the Kyongsang and Cholla
provinces goes back to the late Three Kingdoms period when
Silla and Paekche fought against each other. An unfortunate
legacy of the Park era has been the intensification of this
provincial rivalry, and there is no sign today that the
struggle is about to be mitigated. Again, we hope for
statesmanship but we cannot be very optimistic.

We are not going to answer very many questions today
regarding the reasons for the Kwangju tragedy. That will
require several dissertations or books. But the panelists
here have provided some valuable leads for future scholars.

THE EFFECTS OF THE KWANGJU INCIDENT

Mark Peterson's paper is a major contribution not only
because he elicited new information from Ambassador William
Gleysteen and General John Wickham but also because he tried
to analyze the role of the United States in the Kwangju
incident. The Kwangju incident certainly triggered or
abetted anti-American feelings in certain sectors of the
Korean population. Gleysteen, the former U.S. ambassador to
Korea, attributes anti-Americanism to a "myth" that sprang
up to the effect that the U.S. was partially responsible for
the Kwangju incident. I sympathize with Gleysteen's view,
as cited by Peterson, that "Frustrated by our limited
influence and ignorant of what was going on, the U.S.
government in Seoul and Washington immediately deplored the
violence and encouraged a peaceful settlement."

The rise in anti-Americanism among some Koreans,
however, is not solely because of what the U.S. command in

Seoul did or did not do vis-a-vis the Special Forces or the R.O.K. Army Twentieth Division in May 1980. It has to do with the way the Reagan Administration has treated General Chun since Kwangju. It should be recalled that President Reagan welcomed President Chun Doo Hwan to the White House in February 1981 as his first foreign guest. That symbolic act, so soon after Kwangju, touched the raw nerves of many Koreans. The welcome President Reagan extended was not a case of the U.S. working with the coup "because they saw no reasonable alternative." Though that might have been the situation in the American Embassy in Seoul in 1979-80, it was not the case in Washington in 1981. History may record that the anger against the United States has been proportionate to the degree of warmth which the U.S. government has shown toward the Chun Doo Hwan regime.

We know, of course, that the Kennedy Administration did work with General Park in 1961-62, and that President Kennedy likewise greeted Park at the White House. But Kennedy drove a hard bargain with Park vis-a-vis democracy and Reagan was no Kennedy. Reagan treated Chun as an ally --even a hero.

Another side of anti-Americanism was graphically presented by Linda Lewis. She says the people in Kwangju had an initial expectation of U.S. support but they were later distressed by its absence. Lewis' observation touches on a very complex psychological aspect of U.S.-Korean relations.

All East Asians, be they Chinese, Japanese, Korean or Vietnamese, have put their Big Brothers on pedestals and have traditionally expected them to behave like Big Brothers. At various times when the Americans, Chinese (in the North Korean and Vietnamese context), and Russians have not performed their expected roles, the Asians have felt betrayed. Here we see a cultural gap. To the Westerners, international relations are simply a means of pursuing self-interest. But to East Asians, international relations are an extension of the "five relationships" that Confucius expounded. It is true that Asians are now becoming more and more "Westernized," or realistic. But the change has been slow. Western powers should pay more attention to this aspect of Asian international relations.

THE KWANGJU INCIDENT IN HISTORICAL PERSPECTIVE

The Kwangju incident has already played an important role in the politics of Korea. I detect a subtle change in the attitude of Korean and American soldiers toward politics and I feel that the events in Kwangju are an important reason for this. I also detect a change in the American attitude toward Korean politics. Assistant Secretary of State Gaston Sigur's speech of February 6, 1987 was a major departure for the Reagan Administration in its public stance toward the Korean government, and I have a feeling that Washington is beginning to learn the lessons of Kwangju. I agree with Vincent Brandt's comment at the Asian Studies session in Boston that the Kwangju incident was a major watershed in student attitudes toward the government, the military, communism, etc. There is no doubt that the government lost credibility because it mishandled the Kwangju incident.

I believe, however, the Kwangju incident will have a great influence on the future of Korea--and on how historians look back on the events of the last years of the twentieth century. The scar inflicted by the Kwangju incident on Korean politics is deep and wide. Though it is a page in Korean history that many would rather forget, they will not be able to do so. While it is going to be painful to recount the events of May 1980, the wound will not be healed unless the sins committed in Kwangju are atoned for and forgiven. I believe the panel members made a significant contribution to this end by examining the Kwangju uprising with sympathy for the victims but also with much objectivity.

Document: Report on the Kwangju Incident to the National Assembly National Defense Committee, June 7, 1985

Yoon Sung-min,
Minister of Defense, Republic of Korea

THE BACKGROUND AND THE MOTIVES

My report on the background of the Kwangju incident and the motives behind it is based on announcements by the Martial Law Command in 1980 and the materials collected at the time.

[After] the October 26 incident (the assassination of President Park Chung Hee in 1979), the government . . . promised amnesty and the restoration of civil rights (for politicians and student activists) and curtailed the Martial Law schedule to ensure democratic progress.

Impatient demands by some political forces and instigation by some students fueled campus disturbances to the extent that it was difficult to maintain security nationwide.

Economically, many business firms suffered sit-in demonstrations and sabotage as employer-employee conflicts flared up.

The Sabuk incident (a prolonged radical strike of coal miners) caused a sudden decline in exports and production. It also added to political, economic and social chaos and pushed up commodity prices, threatening the people's livelihood.

North Korea, which was looking for an opportunity to invade the south, was encouraged to moved armored forces closer to the Demilitarized Zone on a large scale.

[O Chin-u], the people's armed forces minister of North Korea, was standing by in the minister's situation room,

This report is taken in full from the **The Korea Herald** (Seoul), June 9, 1985, with minor grammatical corrections.

watching developments in the South. [O Kung-yol], chairman of the Joint Chiefs of Staff, was stationed in southernmost Kaesong. As the military tension increased, our national security and survival was threatened both from within and without.

To make a bad matter worse, the world political situation was rapidly changing as a result of the Iranian and Afghan incidents and conflicts in the Middle East, and intelligence said North Korea would soon attack the South.

As a great majority of people, faced with the greatest crisis since the foundation of the nation, demanded that social well-being and order be restored, the government was forced to take the emergency measures of May 17 (military crackdown on politicians) to face the national difficulties.

Thanks to these measures, peace was restored in most areas, including Seoul. But in Kwangju, student demonstrators took to the street May 19, one day after Martial Law was declared.

Although it was Sunday, about 200 Chonnam National University students, influenced by some political forces, attempted to enter the library with bags filled with stones. When stopped by Martial Law Command troops, the students threw stones at the soldiers in ripple attacks. The Martial Law troops were hit by the stones. Afterwards, the students infiltrated downtown areas for demonstrations in the streets.

The police did their best to restore order, but 27 policemen sustained injuries from demonstrators.

As it was impossible for [the] police to bring the situation under control under the circumstances, troops had to be called in to maintain order.

Clashes between demonstrators and Martial Law troops led to misunderstandings. Groundless rumors fabricated by impure elements deepened regional acrimony, set apart civilians and troops and led to arson, destruction, killings and injuries.

At last, demonstrators seized weapons and armed themselves with the weapons, turning Kwangju to a state of lawlessness and anarchy as the city's administrative functions were paralyzed.

The Supreme Court made it clear that some political forces pulled a string for the flareup of the Kwangju incident.

DEVELOPMENT OF THE INCIDENT

Now I will report on day-by-day developments.

About 200 Chonnam National University students, who clashed with Martial Law Command troops at 9 a.m. in front of the university, advanced to downtown areas of Kwangju at 10 a.m. and demanded that Martial Law be abolished.

The demonstration became more intense as the number of demonstrators increased to about 1,000 by 2:00 p.m. They threw stones at policemen, and set police cars on fire. It was no longer possible for police to bring the situation under control.

The Martial Law authorities attempted at 4:40 p.m. to put an early end to the forceful resistance with part of a military force stationed in the Kwangju area.

Most student demonstrators, however, responded with stone throwing and other means of violence. Some citizens, instigated by groundless rumors, joined the students in throwing stones at troops, resulting in injuries on both sides.

Young soldiers, carrying out their duty in military turmoil, had to arrest student demonstrators while citizens were watching. It was a situation in which there were more or less fierce clashes. But up to then, no one had been killed.

Rumors said, however, "Kyongsang-do soldiers have come to annihilate Cholla-do people," and "They have selected only Kyongsang-do soldiers." and so on.

This was a planned act by impure elements who intended to encourage the internal division and disturbance into a forceful riot.

The soldiers ordered into Kwangju were some of those stationed in the Kwangju area and the 33rd and 35th battalions of the Seventh Airborne Corps in the Chonju area.

The commander of the 33rd battalion was a Chonju native while the commander of the 35th battalion was a Taegu native. About 40 percent of the troops were from Cholla-namdo and Cholla-pukto.

All these facts show how groundless the rumors were.

More rumors spread on May 19, and a mob psychology lacking reason and composure prevailed in Kwangju.

Some agitated demonstrators threw Molotov cocktails at police boxes and set press vans and other vehicles afire. In the turmoil, some demonstrators seized weapons from Martial Law troops for the first time.

Rumors, fabricated from time to time, spread orally or in printed materials in a systematic manner. They said the airborne troops would "kill every young man," and that they intended to "kill 70 percent of Kwangju citizens."

Amid shouts and smoke, demonstrators wielded sticks and iron pipes against police and Martial Law troops resulting in the first two killings.

Little violence was reported on the morning of May 20 when it rained. In the afternoon, however, about 10,000 angry citizens took to the streets again for demonstrations.

Around 4:30 p.m. some 40 taxi drivers, apparently agitated by groundless rumors, gathered on a plaza in front of the Mudung Stadium and began a car demonstration. The number of drivers who joined in the car protest increased to about 20 by 6:30 p.m.

Meanwhile, some violent demonstrators set fire to the Kwangju MBC [Munhwa Broadcasting Company] building and destroyed City Hall and several police substations in downtown areas. Some others roamed the city aboard taxis and buses. Four policemen were killed by the cars in front of the provincial government office building. The reckless drivers also attempted to break through police and military cordons.

Amid such reckless activities, Kwangju turned into a city of terror as arson and other crimes were committed everywhere. An estimated 100,000 citizens participated in various demonstrations and rallies during the day.

Violent demonstrations continued through the night. Some spread unfounded rumors through loudspeakers while roaming the city by car. Some demonstrators carried torches.

Around 11 p.m. the MBC building was burnt down and two Martial Law soldiers were killed in front of the Kwangju Station about 45 minutes later.

Some rioters attacked and set fire to the Kwangju Tax Office at 2 a.m. on May 21. Some others robbed 17 carbine rifles from an armory for reservist troops.

The wayward rioters set the Kwangju Station and the Kwangju KBS [Korea Broadcasting System] building on fire around 6:00 a.m. They also seized whatever cars they found on streets.

At 9:00 a.m. they attacked the Asia Motor Company and took by force some 200 cars, including armored vehicles for military use. With the cars they had stolen, the rioters advanced as far as [the] nearby towns [of] Hwasun, Naju, Tamyang and Changsong and attacked armories there. With face masks, some rioters attacked a mine in Hwasun and the

Kwangju distribution office of Korea Explosives Co and [stole] a large amount of explosives and about 350,000 detonators.

From around 1:00 p.m. on the same day, some installed a machine gun on the roof of a high-story building and fired at Martial Law troops. They attacked the Kwangju Penitentiary, whose inmates included North Korean spies, three times during the day by using the armored vehicles they had robbed. They exchanged fire with the Martial Law Command troops who tried to defend the prison. Fifty-four casualties were reported from the exchange of fire at the penitentiary and other violent incidents during the day.

The rebels also convinced innocent citizens to join them. They published an underground paper in which they incited the citizens to collaborate for the repulsion of the troops.

The rioters attacked not only public buildings but private businesses. At around noon, some of them broke an electric shop, destroyed the goods and set fire to the store. Many service stations were also attacked.

A mob attacked an armory of a police substation in Naju and took 770 rifles, including 510 carbines, and some 110,000 rounds of ammunition. Thus, the rioters became a large-scale rebellious armed group.

They also spread a rumor about the resignation of then Prime Minister [Shin Hyon-hwak] and all cabinet ministers on the day. They alleged that the cabinet resigned, yielding to their brave struggle.

They continued to rouse innocent citizens by falsely saying that then President [Ch'oe Kyu-ha] would also soon resign. And they showed signs that they would intensify their struggle against the Martial Law troops.

In order not to cause innocent loss of life and property, the Martial Law troops withdrew to outlying areas of the city around 6 p.m. In the process some troops were attacked by gun-firing rioters.

After withdrawing to the outlying areas, the troops cut communications and traffic between the city and outside. While suppressing disturbances in other areas, the Martial Law Command tried to persuade the rioters in Kwangju to cease their rebellion. The fierce resistance on the part of the rioters continued. A group of rioters, for instance, attacked some Martial Law troops which had withdrawn to the suburbs of the city. With the entire Kwangju city under the control of the armed rebels, disturbances spread to Yonggwang, Hampyong, Wando, Mokpo, Songjong, Haenam and other parts of Cholla-namdo on May 22.

Rioters attacked the Kwangju Penitentiary again at 9:35 a.m. and exchanged fire with the defending troops.

To block the reentrance of the Martial Law Command troops into the city, the rioters established barricades and encampments along major routes. They prepared for a protracted fight against the troops by organizing what they called the "civilian army."

Rioters displayed dead bodies on the plaza in front of the provincial government office and mobilized innocent citizens on the pretext of holding a funeral.

Then they instigated the citizens to join in the fight against the Martial Law troops. Some of the rioters committed murders and robberies out of personal grudges. Witnessing such cruel behavior of the rioters, many citizens began to feel threatened and started to return to their senses.

On May 23, the situation in the city began to calm down partly due to the efforts by the Martial Law Command to dissuade the rioters from committing any further violent acts. The change of attitude on the part of many students and citizens also contributed to the calm.

However, armed attacks and plunders continued in areas other than Kwangju. In Kwangju, the rioters installed barricades along major routes and established an arms supply base in a park.

Thirty-four rioters surrendered to the Martial Law Command around 7 p.m. A group of citizens also visited the headquarters of the troops and returned some of the weapons they had collected. Thus, there seemed to appear signs that the incident would be resolved through dialogue.

However, such efforts to solve the incident peacefully failed because of the incalcitrant attitude of some hard-core rioters.

These rioters in particular have continued to resist and circulate rumors, such as "the U.S. Seventh Fleet is anchored at Pusan port to support Kwangju citizens" and riots are taking place everywhere in the country in support of the uprising in Kwangju.

On May 24, the rioters began to intensify their resistance. Around 12:30 p.m., they held a citizens' rally, attended by about 15,000 persons, under the pretext of holding a memorial service in front of the building of the Cholla-namdo provincial government. During the rally, they burnt effigies.

On the outskirts of the city, the group of rioters fired against the Martial Law Command troops. There was no sign of an early settlement . . . in view of such acts.

On May 25, the activities of the Settlement Committee made no progress due to the differing opinions of doves and hawks. The hawks in the committee sponsored a citizens' rally which was attended by about 50,000, calling for the abolition of the Martial Law.

As the general citizens began to lose sympathy for the rioters, rebels roused (the ordinary citizens), alleging: "The Martial Law Command troops cannot enter (the city). Everything's O.K. if we endure for five days more. The situation is developing in our favor. (You) citizens join our citizens' troop to fight for the final victory."

As the Martial Law Command troops began to press the siege in some areas on May 26, one day before the troops seized control of the city, the armed rioters were quick to deploy rebel forces. Furthermore, the rioters demonstrated a rapid mobilization under a systematized commanding operation.

They (the rioters) instigated the citizens to rise up and to resist, alleging that the Martial Law Command troops were ready to enter the city by force. They braved the street marching and held a rally at around 3 p.m. by inciting about 5,000 persons.

In reviewing the process and developments of the nine-day incident, one sees the problem was touched off by a fierce street demonstration which started first by the throwing of stones by some students of Chonnam National University at the Martial Law Command troops, and by a clash (between the troops and demonstrators).

The situation became extremely worse as the impure elements which were manipulated by well-organized outside forces stimulated the Kwangju citizens by rousing regional sentiments while circulating rumors.

THE ARMED SUPPRESSION OF THE DISTURBANCE

In the face of the anarchy created by armed rioters, the military refrained from exercising the right of self-defense for fear that citizens might be hurt. Even when soldiers were taken and killed by mobs, the military devoted itself to preventing a worse situation.

Martial Law Command troops were withdrawn to the outskirts of Kwangju May 21, 1980 lest their continued confrontation with rioters should further incite citizens. The troops encircled the city, watching citizens make their own efforts to save the situation.

Upon his appointment as acting prime minister on May 22, [Pak Chung-hun] arrived in Kwangju and issued a statement, appealing to the citizens to calm down and show self-control.

On May 25, 1980, then-President [Ch'oe Kyu-ha] went to Kwangju and issued a special statement in which he entreated the citizens to show self-control and restore order.

The commander of the Martial Law Command dispersed 420,000 copies of printed warnings that those who held weapons, ammunition and explosives might be seen as rebels.

Airplanes and vehicles were used in making continued efforts to persuade citizens to calm down. Such efforts, however, fell short of bringing any result.

Mobsters prepared for the worst, holding huge amounts of TNT in strongholds on the compound of the provincial government office. They created an atmosphere of terror in which citizens were forced to wage protracted warfare. As anarchy continued, those in low-income brackets faced a short supply of daily necessities and medical supplies. There was a danger that collective crimes might be committed.

The government could not expect the citizens to save the situation and restore order for themselves.

As a result of the protracted anarchy, there was an increasing possibility that impure elements or armed North Korean commandos might infiltrate Kwangju.

On the sixth day of the commotion, good citizens began to show signs of calming down, and it became possible to distinguish armed rioters from good citizens.

The military concluded that conditions were ripe for quenching the disturbance with the least possible sacrifice. Military operations were launched at 1 a.m. May 27, 1980 to save the citizens from anarchy.

GUIDELINES FOR MILITARY OPERATIONS

The conditions of lawlessness called for operations similar to regular street fighting. The following guidelines were provided to protect the lives and properties of citizens and to minimize the damages. The guidelines were that sacrifices on both sides should be minimized. Surprise operations should be launched based on correct intelligence to take hold of targets. Persistent efforts were made to retrieve seized weaponry and to encourage the citizens to calm down.

To carry out operations with the least possible sacrifice, Martial Law Command troops took aerial pictures of the Kwangju area, infiltrated agents into Kwangju to locate the deployments of mobsters, and found out the level of their alertness. A potential explosion was prevented by defusing explosives placed in the basement of the provincial government office building in cooperation with good students.

Telephone lines connecting Kwangju with other parts of the nation were disconnected.

Operations were launched at 1 a.m. when citizens were in bed. Troops infiltrated mobsters' encampments in threes and fours secretly to preclude possible [harm] to citizens.

Mobsters offered systematic resistance, and unavoidably 17 armed rioters were killed. The military did its best to minimize the sacrifice in the course of operations.

DAMAGE AND ACTION AGAINST RIOTERS

The death toll resulting from the incident was 191. The fatality figure breaks down to 164 civilians, 23 soldiers an four police officers killed. The seriously wounded came to 122 and the slightly injured to 730, most of whom returned home after simple medical treatment.

The government paid funeral expenses for those killed in the incident. Donations were also given to the bereaved families to comfort them and subsidize their livelihood. The government also paid for the medical treatment of those wounded. Those seriously wounded were given consolation money.

The incident caused 26 billion won in damages, 250 buildings, 882 vehicles, 884 facilities, 3,000 drums of petroleum and 1,925 items of equipment were either destroyed or burned.

The government fully restored destroyed houses and buildings and made proper compensation for damaged equipment and materials.

Rioters seized or looted 5,008 military rifles, 395 shotguns, 288,680 rounds of ammunition, 562 hand grenades and 3,000 boxes of explosives. The government retrieved 4,926 rifles or 98 percent of the 5,008 lost rifles.

Arrested in connection with the Kwangju incident were 2,522 people, 1,906 of whom were released after receiving admonitions. Four hundred and four were court-martialed and sentenced to various prison terms while the charges against 212 were dropped.

Those in prison in connection with the Kwangju incident were released and now there are no prisoners connected with the incident.

CONCLUSION

This has been a comprehensive report of the Kwangju incident. I think you, Assemblymen, have a good understanding of the incident. I would like to make it clear that this report is true and correct.

Circulating rumors concerning the death toll resulting from the incident are groundless for the following reasons.

First, reports of deaths were received for 10 days after the disturbance was settled. There were no fatality reports other than the 164 civilian deaths.

Second, the number of deaths were confirmed by a team of 49 coroners picked from among medical doctors, lawyers, prosecutors, military coroners and citizens.

Third, the Kwangju City government provided the bereaved families with 14,300,000 won per death. There were no families besides the 164 who claimed the money.

Fourth, five years have passed since the incident. Bereaved families, relatives, human rights organizations and other agencies have made no additional reports of deaths.

There are rumors that the death toll resulting from the incident exceeds 2,000. These rumors seem to originate from the fact that an estimated 2,000 people were reported either killed or missing at that time.

The figure, however, includes those killed, detained, hospitalized and others.

If there are fatalities other than 164 deaths, I request them to be reported to the government, the Assembly, major political parties, news media organizations, religious organizations, social and human rights organizations.

The Kwangju incident was a great national crisis. I think no one can dispute the fact that the military played a decisive role in protecting the nation from this crisis.

Therefore, I entreat you, Assemblymen, to cooperate in the prevention of a further lowering of the morale of the military in connection with the Kwangju incident.

This has been a report of all aspects of the Kwangju incident.

Document: ROK Units Under Operational Control of the Combined Forces Command

FACT SHEET

Public Affairs Office
United Nations Command/Combined Forces Command
United States Forces Korea/Eighth United States Army
APO 96301

FACT 1: Command authority of ROK Armed Forces always remains with the ROK Government as a function of national sovereignty. However, operational control (OPCON) of ROK Armed Forces by the ROK-US Combined Forces Command (CFC) is a specific delegation of control over ROK forces for purposes of meeting missions entrusted to CFC by both governments.

FACT 2: Operational Control (OPCON) is a standard military relationship regulating tactical control of forces for specific purposes or missions. The specific agreement or treaty that establishes OPCON may change, as occurred in Korea when the ROK-US Combined Forces Command (CFC) assumed the defense mission from the United Nations Command (UNC) in 1978; however, the military relationship itself is unchanged unless specifically modified by pertinent authorities. In Korea, no modifications were or are in force.

FACT 3: The agreement under which ROK military forces are assigned under CFC's OPCON is called the "Terms of Reference for the Military Committee and ROK-US Combined Forces Command," dated July 27, 1978. This is a binational agreement which established the mission, organization, functions and command relationships under which the Republic of Korea and the United States control military forces in Korea.

This document, issued in Seoul, is an official statement of the Combined Forces Command's position on the issue of operational control (OPCON) by the American Commander-in-Chief.

FACT 4: [The Commander-in-Chief of the Combined Forces Command] CINCCFC has OPCON of forward positioned ROK Forces including air for the external defense of the ROK.

Fact 5: Should the ROK Government have need to recover OPCON of a specific force from the CFC, the normal practice has been that the Chairman, ROK Joint Chiefs of Staff would notify Commander-in-Chief, CFC (CINCCFC), by letter. In an emergency situation, notification could take place by the most expedient means, such as military communications channels. Although the CINCCFC is obligated by the nature of his responsibilities to inform the ROK Government [ROKG] on all matters affecting external defense readiness, there is no provision in the binational agreement which would allow him to refuse to comply with the ROKG's decision.

FACT 6: CINCCFC is not an official party to the ROKG's use of its national forces once they are withdrawn from CFC's OPCON.

FACT 7: In December 1979, the ROK Government did not request release of the 9th Division or the one regiment of the division which actually moved, prior to movement. CINCCFC received official notificvation late the afternoon of Dec. 13 and the change of OPCON to the ROK Government was made official as of 12:01 a.m. Dec. 14.

FACT 8: The ROK Army forces that were initially involved in Kwangju in 1980 were not subordinate in any way to CFC. When the ROK Government decided to replace these forces with a unit of the 20th Division, it notified the CINCCFC in advance.

END

Selected Readings

Dong, Wonmo, ed. Korean-American Relations at Crossroads. Princeton, N.J.: The Association of Korean Christian Scholars in North America, 1982.

Gleysteen, William H., "Korea: A Special Target of American Concern," in David D. Newsom, ed. The Diplomacy of Human Rights. Lanham, Md.: University Press of America, 1986, pp. 85-99.

Henderson, Gregory. "American Command in Korea: The Political Dangers." Unpublished paper, Conference on Korea in the Shadow of the Philippines: Democratization and the United States, February 13-14 1987.

Human Rights in Korea. New York and Washington, D.C.: The Asia Watch Committee, 1986.

Hwang So-gyong. Chugumul nomo, sidaeui odumul nomo (Over Death, Over the Darkness of the Age). Washington, D.C.: The Capital Union Presbyterian Church for Koreans, 1985.

Kim, Chi-ha. The Middle Hour: Selected Poems of Kim Chi Ha. tr. David R. McCann. Stanfordville, N.Y.: Human Rights Publishing Group, 1980.

Kim, Dae Jung. Prison Writings. tr. David R. McCann and Sung-il Choi. Berkeley, Calif.: University of California Press, 1987.

Kim, Quee-young. _The Fall of Syngman Rhee_. Berkeley, Calif.:
    University of California Press, 1983.

Kwon, Kyongmi, comp. _Cholladoyo, Cholladoyo_ (O Cholla
    Province, O Cholla Province). Seoul: Osangsa
    Publishers, 1985.

Lee, Chong-Sik. _The Politics of Korean Nationalism_.
    Berkeley, Calif.: University of California Press, 1963.

Lee, Peter H. _Anthology of Korean Literature_. Honolulu:
    University of Hawaii Press, 1981.

Lee, Suk Bok. _The Impact of U.S. Forces in Korea_.
    Washington, D.C.: National Defense University, 1987.

Korea May 1980: People's Uprising in Kwangju. Tokyo:
    Pacific-Asia Resources Center, 1980.

Perry, Elizabeth J. _Rebels and Revolutionaries in North
    China, 1845-1945_. Stanford: Stanford University Press,
    1980.

Reports from Kwangju. Washington, D.C.: North American
    Coalition for Human Rights in Korea, n.d.

Republic of Korea. Korean Overseas Information Service.
    Kwangju Turmoil--Facts vs. Rumors. Seoul: Korean
    Overseas Information Service, 1980.

Republic of Korea. Korean Overseas Information Service.
    Nationwide Martial Law--Background and Necessity.
    Seoul: Korean Overseas Information Service, 1980.

Rhee, Taek-hyung, _US-ROK Combined Operations: a Korean
    Perspective_. Washington, D.C.: National Defense
    University, 1986.

Shaplen, Robert. "Letter from South Korea," _The New Yorker_.
    November 17, 1980.

So, Chong-ju. _Unforgettable Things_. tr. David R. McCann.
    Seoul: Si-sa-yong-o-sa, 1987.

Warnberg, Tim. "The Kwangju Uprising: an Inside View."
    Korean Studies. XI (1987). Forthcoming.

Contributors

Donald N. Clark is Associate Professor of History at Trinity University in San Antonio and the author of Christianity in Modern Korea (1986).

David R. McCann is Adjunct Associate Professor of Asian Studies at Cornell University. His latest work is a translation of the poems of So Chong-ju entitled Unforgettable Things (1986).

Linda Lewis is Assistant Professor of Anthropology at Amherst College. She is finishing a book entitled Compromising Justice: Mediation and Judicial Process in a Korean Court.

Mark Peterson is Assistant Professor of East Asian Languages and Civilizations at Brigham Young University and the co-editor of Korean Women: View from the Inner Room (1983).

Chong-Sik Lee is Professor of Political Science at the University of Pennsylvania. His most recent book is Japan and Korea: the Political Dimension (1985).

Index